speaking of
Jesus

50 Easy Ways to #sharejesus

carl medearis

 simply for students

JESUS–CENTERED

Guide your entire ministry toward a passionate Jesus-centered focus with this series of innovative resources. Harness the power of these dynamic tools that will help you draw teenagers and leaders into a closer orbit around Jesus.

Speaking of Jesus: Student Edition

group.com
simplyyouthministry.com

CREDITS
Author: Carl Medearis
Executive Developer: Tim Gilmour
Chief Creative Officer: Joani Schultz
Editors: Rick Lawrence and Rob Cunningham
Cover Art and Art Director: Veronica Preston
Original Cover Design for *Speaking of Jesus*: Amy Konyndyk
Production Artist: Joyce Douglas
Project Manager: Stephanie Krajec

ISBN 978-1-4707-2693-5

10 9 8 7 6 5 4 3 2 1   21 20 19 18 17 16 15

Printed in the United States of America.

Contents

Introduction

One Sunday a pastor wanted to use a squirrel as an object lesson for the children in his Sunday school class. "I'm going to describe something, and I want you to raise your hand when you know what it is," explained the pastor. The children nodded eagerly. "This thing lives in trees (pause) and eats nuts (pause)..." No hands went up. "It's gray (pause) and has a long bushy tail (pause)..." The children looked at each other nervously, but still nobody raised a hand. "It jumps from branch to branch (pause) and chatters and flips its tail when it's excited (pause)..."

Finally one little boy tentatively raised his hand. The pastor quickly called on him. "Well," said the boy, "I *know* the answer must be 'Jesus,' but it sure sounds like a squirrel!"

It seems to me that we all are a little like that boy—we know the answer is Jesus. We believe it. We say it. But the way we describe Jesus sounds scripted, and often doesn't match the Jesus revealed in the Bible. I hope that in the following pages I can help you overcome that.

I remember the horribly awkward moments of my teenage years. My friend would ask me to come to his house to hang out on Sunday morning and I had to tell him "No." Why? "Because I go to church." Ugh.

Once, in sixth grade, my science teacher was going on and on about evolution—he said that if you believed in "creation" you must be some kind of idiot. To be honest, I wasn't sure exactly what I believed about that—but I didn't like his tone.

So as terrified as I was, I cleared my throat, thrust my hand in the air, and mumbled something incoherent like, "I do." The teacher asked, "I do WHAT?" I think I'd forgotten to connect "I do" with anything specific. "Uh," I said, "I believe in God." And I'll never forget his response: "Well, congratulations. Does anyone else here believe in GAWD?" Of course, several of my friends did, but guess what? Not one of them raised a hand, and I went down on my very own private sinking ship. I'm still not a big fan of science-class teachers...

Now that I think of it, I could probably fill this book with similarly embarrassing scenarios. You know the type of situation. You've been there, lived that. You tried to be brave and got shot down. So the next time you chickened out, only to feel awful about it later.

There has to be a better way, right?

There must be a way to talk to others about the most important relationship in your life without getting a graduate degree or channeling C.S. Lewis or some other great Christian thinker. There must be a way to share Jesus with your friends and family and people you meet that won't kill you with embarrassment—at least not every time! There must be a way to have a conversation about Jesus that makes sense. That relates. That is honest and fair and kind and gentle, yet strong and firm and real.

So I suggest we follow the way of Jesus. Maybe you've missed the simplicity of Jesus' way. It's sometimes bold and brash, but other times it's so gentle that you miss it. It's inviting. At times, it's fun and even playful. It hints and suggests and only beats you over the head with "truth" if you're a religious zealot. Otherwise, the way of Jesus simply invites you to come to him. And your friends will come. Many will come. Maybe all of them. I'd assume nothing less.

So, no guilt. No five points. No six diagrams.

Let's speak of Jesus.

And another thing...

Because "sharing Jesus" with your friends and enemies and frenemies is the point of this book, at the end of each these 50 ideas I've given you a short (140 characters or less) #sharejesus nugget that you can post on Twitter or Facebook or Instagram. Or, alternatively, I guess you could hire a pilot to sky-write each #sharejesus nugget. Your call.

PART 1:
Knowing Jesus

If you're reading this, you now know me. At least, you know my name. You may have heard someone recommend "this book by Carl Medearis" and so you picked it up. Or maybe someone who cares about you, and knows something about me, decided to give you this book. At the very least, after you're done reading this book, if someone asks if you know "that Medearis guy," you could answer "yes." Fair enough.

But not really.

You don't know me. You don't know what really motivates and drives me. What lies beneath the big outer shell. How I treat my wife and kids. You don't even *really* know if my great stories are totally true. Maybe I made them up. You don't know my deepest dreams and desires, or if I'd want to have coffee with you sometime to talk about them. You know me, but not really...

And so it is with us whenever we say we "know Jesus." We might know him because we've gone to church all our life, or we read the Bible from time to time. We might even know him as our Lord and Savior (a good idea, by the way). So we believe in Jesus. That's good. But do you believe what Jesus believed? What *did* he believe? What were his dreams and passions and goals? Why did he talk to some people one way, and others in a totally different way? Not just what did Jesus do, but *why* did he do it? Does he consume your mind and heart? Do you wake up with him on your mind and drift off at night thinking about him?

If not, you can. And when you do, it'll change everything.

1: Know Nothing But Jesus

I'm going to make this book-reading thing really easy. If you remember just one sentence from this entire book, this is it:

During all my years of sharing my faith with others, I've learned that there's really only one thing that's important, and that is Jesus himself.

Yup, that's it. The most important sentence in this book.

Obviously, I still want you to keep reading because we're going to talk about a lot of other important, relevant things. But it all comes back to that one, simple idea: knowing Jesus.

I often have to force myself to remember the straightforward resolution of the Apostle Paul: "For I resolved to know nothing while I was with you except Jesus Christ and him crucified" (1 Corinthians 2:2). Life for Paul was all about simply knowing nothing else but Jesus. I know the one place I can't go wrong is the place where Jesus is. I can be weak, sinful, foolish, and even rebellious. I can fail others, foul up my relationships, and fumble my work—and still, I can't go wrong when I'm determined to know only Jesus Christ.

If you and I hung out with Paul, he would talk about one thing above all. He would speak of Jesus. If Paul could make one declaration to those of us who call ourselves Christians today, he would simply plead with us to stick close to Jesus. He would say, "Get this: There is one thing that matters above all. Jesus Christ."

That's why I believe in speaking "of Jesus," not "about Jesus."

Paul wrote that he "preached Christ," not "about Christ" (1 Corinthians 1:23). What's the difference? I talk *about* Denver Broncos football because I'm not exactly on the team. I talk *about* politics because I'm not exactly a politician. But I speak *of* Jesus because I'm "in" him. I only speak *of* the things that I know from the inside out. Do we know him? Really know him? If we do, then we can speak *of* Jesus, not *about* Jesus.

Those of us who are followers of Jesus know the creator firsthand. You could even say we're BFFs with the King. We know where truth is found, and we know its name. We know what brings life and what gives life and where eternal life can be found. If you think about it, it really isn't fair. While others are explaining and defending various "isms" and "ologies," we're simply pointing people to our friend: the One who uncovers and disarms, the beginning and the end of the story.

What if we were to take Jesus at his word: "And I, if I am lifted up from the earth, will draw all peoples to Myself" (John 12:32, NKJV)? What if our complicated explanations about the Bible and the Christian life are wrong, not because they are incorrect, but because they do not primarily focus on the person of Jesus?

#sharejesus:

I believe in speaking "of Jesus," not "about Jesus."
I only speak of the things that I know from the inside out.

2. Read About Jesus

I grew up with a kind of "Navy SEALs" mindset about the Bible—the tougher the better. So I camped a lot in the Old Testament, and pored over what the Apostle Paul had to say. For some reason, the Gospel accounts of Jesus' ministry on earth felt like the background story to the good stuff. You know, Hebrews and Romans and Galatians and then that crazy book of Revelation (once you reach mega-mature status).

I didn't spend a lot of time in Matthew, Mark, Luke, and John. And when I did, it was mostly in John. The synoptic Gospels (the first three) didn't have much theology in them—just a lot of stories about Jesus doing stuff, plus parables that seemed odd and confusing to me. I wanted the meaty stuff. *Of course, of course, we need the Gospels to give us the basics—yeah, Jesus died and rose again—but then let's move on as fast as possible to the stuff we can really sink our teeth into: "thick" ideas like justification, atonement, salvation, and redemption.* Looking back, I was more interested in the recipes of Jesus than the cook himself—it all seems funny when I think about it now.

Today I tell people that if you want to get to know Jesus, the actual person, then read the four Gospels. Read them until they become part of you. Eat and breathe them. That's what I did for a long season in the mid-'90s—I read nothing but the Gospels for several years. I mean it—I never strayed outside the accounts of what Jesus actually said and did for a very long time. And even then, I felt like I'd only scratched the surface of Jesus.

Now, don't get distracted or misunderstand my point: I think *all* the books of the Bible are important—all 66 of them. They're all helpful. They're all inspired by God. Together they make up his Word. But two things are called "the Word": the Bible and Jesus. All of Scripture points to him.

I remember hearing a story about the great 19th century British pastor Charles Spurgeon giving feedback to his pastoral intern, at the young man's request, after he'd delivered his first sermon at Spurgeon's church. Spurgeon told the young man that he did a great job, but that he'd missed one key element. The young preacher asked what that was. "There was no Christ in your message, son. We preach Christ here at New Park Street Church." The intern was shocked. "But, sir," he replied, "I was preaching from the book of Ezekiel." Spurgeon responded, "Son, until you can find Christ in Ezekiel you will not share my pulpit again."

Jesus, the Word, became flesh and lived with us. And now dwells in us. All of the Bible is helpful, but it is a signpost to the ultimate Word of God: Jesus, the Christ. We do not follow the Bible. We don't worship the Bible. We love it because it directs us toward the One who is everything. So while all of the Bible is God's Word, it is not all equal in weight. Is Matthew more important to know than

Numbers? Yes. Numbers has its place, and it's part of the story and from God's Spirit, but that doesn't mean it carries the same weight of importance that the Gospel account of Matthew does. I used to think that in order to share my faith effectively, I had to know and defend the entire Bible. Every single word!

Has this ever happened to you? You muster up the courage to finally talk to that person you've wanted to share your faith with, and before you know it, wham! They pull out the clobber questions: *How can you believe that God created the universe in six days when everybody knows the universe is 14 billion years old? What about all those people God commanded the Israelites to kill in the Old Testament? Do you actually believe that a whale swallowed Jonah?*

I feel your pain. It's happened to me, too. I used to get so frustrated, until it dawned on me that I don't have to defend or understand everything in the Bible in order to share my faith. Jesus is the point of the Bible. It all points to him. I don't have to be the Bible's defense attorney. All I have to do is speak of Jesus, and he will draw people to himself. The campground where Jesus lives is in the Gospels, so camp there if you want to get to know him.

#sharejesus:

I don't have to be the Bible's defense attorney. All I have to do is speak of Jesus, and he will draw people to himself.

3. "Eat" Jesus

Here's one of the many ridiculous things Jesus says to people in the Bible—at least, it *seems* ridiculous on the face of it:

> **"I tell you the truth, unless you eat the flesh of the Son of Man and drink his blood, you have no life in you. Whoever eats my flesh and drinks my blood has eternal life, and I will raise him up at the last day. For my flesh is real food and my blood is real drink. Whoever eats my flesh and drinks my blood remains in me, and I in him" (John 6:53-56).**

That's crazy talk. This is exactly the kind of stuff that got Jesus killed. In fact, a few verses later, we see that many of the disciples no longer followed Jesus. This teaching was just too weird. *Is this guy a cannibal, or what?* But in the Gospel of John, Jesus uses "bread" as the primary metaphor to describe himself—he wants us to have the kind of intimate relationship with him that we have with our food.

Think about it. You take something from outside yourself and put it inside yourself. If we weren't so used to eating stuff, we'd be freaked out by the whole thing. It's pretty clear Jesus wants something more than a casual relationship with us. He's inviting us to understand him, not as a theological exercise, but to know him the same way we know what an apple tastes like when we take a big bite. He wants us to inhale him. So exactly how does that work?

I have no idea.

But here are a couple of my best guesses.

First, I think we need to believe that it's possible to have him in us. Really inside of us. Believing that what Jesus asks of us is possible should always be Point Number One. When he heard the disciples grumbling (John 6:60-64), Jesus said that he knew some didn't believe. There's a direct connection between eating Jesus and having faith in Jesus. Maybe they're even the same; I don't know. I know that when I'm consciously aware that Jesus is alive in me right now—at this moment—it helps me to pursue a relationship with him. I often (sometimes several times a day) ask myself this question: "If Jesus were living my life right now and he were here doing what I'm doing, would he be pleased or would he want to do something else?"

I think that's a better question than "What would Jesus do?" We can never be sure what Jesus would do if he were here right now. But we do know what Jesus *did*. So I think we should ask this question: "Based on what Jesus did (which requires me to know some of that), what might he want to do through me right now, since he lives in me?" Or ask it this way: "If Jesus had my life to live today, how would he be living it right now?"

#sharejesus:

Jesus wants us to know him the same way we know what an apple tastes like when we take a big bite. He wants us to inhale him.

4. Practice Acting Like Jesus

I'm not really that good at being Jesus, so my best strategy to get to know him more deeply is to *act like him*. I'm acting. Pretending. But I do it with a deep desire to be like him. That's what I want, because the more I become like him, the more deeply I'll know his heart. But because I'm a knucklehead, I act. Of course, our ultimate dream as Jesus' followers is to really be Christ-like—to have every part of us so in love with Jesus that we find ourselves, almost as an afterthought, becoming like him.

So practice. Practice acting like Jesus. And to live a life like Jesus we must begin by being a student of Jesus. This is the seed of discipleship. Throughout your day, think about the things Jesus said and did in the Gospels. Because I've camped in those four books for such a long time now, the ways Jesus taught and interacted with people in those 89 chapters is basically stored in my brain's hard drive. In any situation, the things he said and did in similar situations just pop into my head. You can't imagine how helpful this is if you haven't done it. But you'll have to know the Gospels better than you did yesterday (and when tomorrow comes, better than you do today). Ask for the Spirit of Jesus who lives in you to teach you about him. After all, that's the Spirit's job description—he's supposed to teach us everything we need to know about Jesus, and "remind you of everything I have said to you" (John 14:26).

If you know Jesus, you'll speak Jesus—so, what do you know about Jesus? He loved to hang out with the outcasts, for example. Who are you hanging out with? Get used to this "acting like Jesus" thing and it'll change your life. We speak of what we know. Know Jesus and you will speak Jesus.

#sharejesus:

Practice acting like Jesus—to live a life like Jesus we must begin by being a student of Jesus. This is the seed of discipleship.

5. Embrace the Mystery of Jesus

Is it possible that those of us who've said we want to follow Jesus don't actually have anything figured out, and we're all just faking it? One of my friends and I were talking about this the other day. He said, "Carl, how come everybody is always ripping on the disciples?" I thought about it for a second.

"You know, probably because they made so many mistakes."

"Yeah—so?" he asked. "See, that's the thing, right there. Everybody assumes that we're somehow superior to Peter and John and the others. We think we're smarter, we think..."

I picked up where he left off. "We think that we wouldn't be as bewildered by Jesus if we were in their shoes."

"Exactly," he said. "Take Peter, for example. Everybody always makes fun of Peter for sinking while trying to walk on the water. We make an example out of him, and we use him to makes points for sermons."

"Yeah, I know," I said, "I heard it a couple of weeks ago. The pastor said, 'Peter sank because he took his eyes off Jesus.' "

"I was just gonna say that," he said, "but do we actually know that's why Peter sank? Anyway, the point is, we spend so much time laughing at Peter for sinking, when in reality, every single one of us would probably have stayed in the boat, right?"

"Absolutely. Matter of fact, I would have tied myself to the mast."

"I'd be right next to you, wetting my pants."

I laughed. "Probably a tunic."

As I was driving home afterward, I realized that our conversation was deeper than I'd realized at first. Something mysterious was swimming around in my head, something I couldn't figure out about Jesus. Typical. He was so confusing to the disciples. Actually, Jesus was confusing to *everybody*. His teachings were so upside down, so unheard of, that he flat-out baffled everybody who listened to him.

After a few days of thinking about it, I realized my friend was making a point I'd been trying to pound home for years. Somehow, we think that because we're "Christians" and because we go to church and because we have the Bible and because we've heard stories and sermons and went to school—we think that makes us smart, sharp, and oh-so-dialed-in. We can't be fooled. We won't be baffled. We would do so much better than the disciples. We would have the plan figured out with a snap of the fingers. Easy as pie, right?

But I think that's a load of junk. And I think it's arrogant, too. I think we forget that Jesus astounded the elders, teachers, and priests in the Temple when he hadn't even hit puberty yet. We forget that Jesus confounded the wise, humbled the intellectuals, and left the educated rocking on their heels with something to think about. One of the first and best steps we can take to know Jesus more deeply is to acknowledge we don't really know very well—right now.

#sharejesus:

We forget that Jesus astounded the religious teachers and priests when he hadn't hit puberty. To know him we first admit we don't know him.

6. Accept Jesus for Who He Is

One key to following Jesus is a little counterintuitive—we must tell ourselves to see him as another person, not some alien from heaven-space. This is exactly how he chose to come to us: as a person born and raised in obscurity and everyday "normal." If we're too quick to put him on a God-pedestal, we unconsciously make it more difficult to know him as he really is. We treat him like an unknowable mystic who says and does strange and otherworldly things. It sounds funny, but a big reason so many people don't know and understand Jesus better is that we over-spiritualize him. Yes, Jesus is God—but set that aside for a bit.

When we accept Jesus as a person first, it makes our experience with him more real. Living with a real person forces us to live honestly. Like in a friendship. Instead of living by some moral code, or conjuring up some spiritual state of mind, all we have to do is make our life about a relationship with a person. God has shortened the distance between us by coming here, and he has made the kingdom of heaven available in friendship form.

By accepting Jesus as a man, we are accepting the invitation of heaven as it is offered to us. If we step away from our conventional ways of seeing Jesus, it will actually require us to trust him. We invite him to explain himself instead of forcing him into the box we've constructed for him. We have, for so many years, used every logical tool in our box to define and explain God—to make him fit our own preconceptions and expectations. We work hard to explain God to ourselves using apologetics and creation science and arguments and doctrines. But Jesus came, specifically, to describe himself to us. Our religious traditions can sometimes be a substitute for letting Jesus define God as he really is.

To do that, we must allow Jesus to be a man.

#sharejesus:

When we accept Jesus as a person first, it makes our experience more real. Living with a real person forces us to live honestly.

7. Follow Jesus Wherever He Goes

Sometimes the people that we think are "furthest away" from Jesus have a greater appreciation for him than those of us "nearest" to him.

I was staying with friends at a hotel in Basra, Iraq, in the spring of 2003. While there, we managed to attract the interest of the hotel staff. They were curious about this team of international people staying at their hotel. Since a war was well underway, they were all the more intrigued because we weren't wearing camouflage and toting M4 carbines. During the day, out in the streets, we had given out all of our texts: Arabic translations of the Gospel of Luke. We were checking in for another day and as we stood in the lobby near the front desk, the hospitality manager leaned across the counter and looked at me.

"Why have you come here?" he asked in English. "Are you with the American army?"

"No," I said, "we followed Jesus to Basra, so we are trying to find out what he is doing here."

He took in his breath with a hiss. "Isa?" he asked, using Muslims' name for Jesus. "Isa is in Basra?"

"We think so," my friend Samir said, "and he wants us to help out in any way we can."

The manager made something like a gasping sound and snatched the phone off the cradle. He rattled off a quick sentence in Arabic, hung up, and came around in front of the desk. "If you please," he said, "stay right here. I know you must be very busy, but I had to call my brother. He loves to hear about Isa."

Samir and I looked at each other. Isa was in Basra after all. Within a few seconds, three other men joined us, all in their 20s or 30s, each wearing the dark blue uniform suit of the hotel staff. For a moment I wondered if they were going to ask us to leave. Then, one of the men, with black hair and a thickening moustache, rushed forward and shook my hand. He moved on down the line, shaking hands vigorously, his eyes lit up like candles.

"You know about Isa?" he asked, returning to me. "Yes," I said, in Arabic. "We followed him here."

"Oh my." His hands shot to his face. "Let me tell you something," he went on. "When I was a young boy, a man came through our city, and he was telling stories about Isa to the people."

The rest of the group and the hotel staff moved closer, listening intently.

"When this man left, he gave my father a cassette tape with recordings of the stories of Isa, the miracles and teachings of Isa, the people he talked to, and how he lived."

"Wow," I said.

"Every night, for 10 years, my father would play the tape for me and my brothers and sisters. He played it until the tape did not work anymore." He stopped for a second, caught his breath. "I love these stories of Isa, and I miss them."

"Well," I said, "we..."

He cut me off, excited. "I have heard, from my father and the old men of the city, they say that there are books, sacred books, ancient books that tell the stories of Isa, as they happened, by the friends of Isa. Is this true?"

"Yes," I said, "and as a matter of fact, we have been giving them out all day."

He almost fainted. I could see his face color, then pale, then color again. He was vibrating with excitement. "Oh please," he said as he gripped my hand, "you must find one for me, you must give me one. I have to have one."

"All right," I said, and turned toward the elevator. "I'll see if I've got one left."

As I rode the elevator up to my room, I realized I was nearly shaking from the same excitement.

I tore my room apart. I ripped open my suitcases and threw my clothes all over the room. A shirt hung from the bathroom doorknob, a pair of socks stuck in the lamp. Finally, after scrabbling around in my luggage like a miner digging for ore, I found one: a Gospel of Luke. In Arabic, the title was something like "the Gospel of Luke, a follower of Jesus." I snatched it, raced out of the room, and rushed for the lobby.

I will never forget his face when I handed it to him. With tears on his cheeks he held it reverently, lifted it to his forehead, and closed his eyes. He lowered it to his lips, gave it a kiss, and then slowly opened it to look at the print. He lovingly ran his fingers over the pages, and then bolted for the lobby desk. He picked up the phone, dialed rapidly, and spoke even faster. When he hung up, he looked at me and said, "I had to call my father; he will know if these are the same stories of Isa as I heard before."

We waited for a few minutes, and after some time an aging Iraqi man showed up—gray beard and all. He looked at us a little suspiciously at first and made his way over to his son, who was literally popping up and down with excitement.

"Papa," he said, "these men have come here because they are followers of Isa. I told them about the stories of Isa on the tape, and asked them if they had heard of the writings of the stories, and they gave me one of them."

The old man came closer, picked up the Gospel, and lifted it to his face. He read the title, thumbed through the pages, pausing to read here and there, and then he stopped, lifted the book to his lips, and kissed it, tears in the corners of his eyes. "Yes," he said, "this is it. These are the stories of Isa." He wrung our hands, hugging us to his body, so grateful that he shook.

We followed Jesus to Basra and found he'd already been there before us. Jesus goes to some pretty strange and unexpected places. You'll come to know him more deeply when you follow him to those strange places. When you read about Jesus in the Gospels, think about the man in Basra who'd heard about Jesus when he was a child, and longed to hear the stories of him again from the rest of his life. Read the stories of Jesus this way, and follow where he goes.

#sharejesus:

Jesus goes to some pretty unexpected places. You'll know him more deeply when you follow him to those places.

8. Stay Focused on Jesus

Jesus didn't come to build a kingdom. He brought one with him. He *is* the kingdom. He's not pointing the way to the door into that kingdom; *he is the door.* When Jesus said, "The kingdom of heaven is at hand" (Matthew 3:2, NKJV), he was saying that we can live in that kingdom right now. *Right now.*

Because Jesus spoke in the outlying regions, not from the pulpit of the Temple, he spread this good news to people who were never likely to get anywhere near the Temple. When he said, "The kingdom of heaven is at hand," heads turned and the whispering started. "Where? Do you see it?"

Wherever he went, the pained and lost people he met followed him. The message Jesus brought to them was that *he was the kingdom of heaven,* and that if you followed him you'd take on an "easy and light yoke." He was available. He was compassionate. And he made house calls.

When we see his first encounter with the brothers Peter and Andrew, Jesus didn't hold a quick meeting to get his objectives out in the open. He didn't garner support or build a ministry team. "Look, here's the plan," Jesus could easily have said. "I came here to die as a sacrifice for the sins of all humanity. When I do that, we're going to build a church, and we're going to reach all the people who are lost in their own sin. All you have to do is believe in me."

But he didn't do that.

When Jesus died, he was broke. His disciples split up, his followers turned on him, and he had to give his mother away to his friend John. Is it any wonder that Satan could overlook someone so low? All of the things that were high and lofty, all of the powerbrokers, all of the political offices and strategic objectives were far from this humble man, this Galilean who spoke about loving enemies and turning the other cheek.

I wonder: Do we overlook him, too?

We have amazing preachers, speakers, and teachers who are very good at describing the standards and practices of the kingdom of heaven. But they often seem to forget that Jesus himself is the kingdom of heaven. Jesus is the message itself—he's not simply the bearer of that message.

#sharejesus:

Jesus didn't come to build a kingdom. He brought one with him. He *is* the kingdom.

9. Take the Cuffs Off

Pretend you're handcuffed to something. The cuffs are tight on your wrists, and the links of chain lace through the bars of a rocking chair. You'd better get used to rocking in that chair, because that's all you'll be able to do until those cuffs come off. Try taking a shower while you're sitting in a rocking chair. Or getting on a school bus. Or playing soccer.

It's not just nearly impossible—if you tried to do any of these things while handcuffed to your rocking chair, you'd become a nuisance. People would raise their eyebrows and sigh as you clunked and scraped and hauled your way up to them. "Hi, guys," you'd pant, breathless. "What's up?" They'd look at each other, pretending not to see your rocking chair. And then they'd have to decide whether or not to mention your predicament, given the obvious embarrassment of it.

Likewise, when we think it's our "job" to tell "lost" people that they can be "saved" by Jesus, we're handcuffing ourselves to a rocking chair. The gospel—the good news—is a person, not a sales presentation. But we have often handcuffed ourselves to a "gospel rocking chair" of traditions, movements, and organizations. We've even handcuffed the simple good news represented by the person of Jesus to a particular society and government. To millions of people around the world, Jesus Christ is synonymous with Western culture and America.

The problem isn't that these attachments are or aren't good; the problem is that these things are not the gospel. Do we really want to try to redefine and reinterpret Jesus and then give him to the world? Of course not. When we handcuff things to Jesus, we are convoluting the message. The power of Jesus' life and death come from a simple truth: He's the exact representation of his Father. Know Jesus and you know God. Do we really want to add to that?

I don't want to redefine salvation or the gospel or even Christianity—I suppose I want to undefine them. I want to strip away the thousands of years of graffiti painted onto the gospel that have turned it into a reasonable code of doctrines. The gospel is not an idea. It is not a belief. It is not a favorite verse. The gospel does not live in your church. It can't be written down in a simple message, and it is not rote prayer. The gospel is not a what. It is not a how. The gospel is a Who. The gospel is literally the good news of Jesus. Jesus is the gospel.

#sharejesus:

The gospel is a person, not a sales presentation. Know Jesus and you know God. Do we really want to add to that?

PART 2:
Sharing Jesus

Everything begins with knowing Jesus. *Really* knowing him. I often say something like this when I'm speaking to a crowd: "Please don't talk about Jesus unless you just can't help it." Obviously, that's sort of a verbal trick, because I do want them (and you) to speak of Jesus—to everyone. But I don't want you to do it because you're supposed to or because someone told you to. Don't share your love for Jesus and your faith in him because "that's what Christians do." Share him because you can't help yourself. Jesus said, "For out of the overflow of the heart the mouth speaks" (Matthew 12:34).

I live in Denver, and I'm a Broncos fan. I've never been to a cheering seminar, but when the Broncos score, I automatically (out of a deep-rooted love) jump up and yell something ridiculous. It just happens. And that's the way it is with Jesus. Yes, we can refine our approach. We can learn some things about how to share this deep passion we have for the One who rescued us. But in the end, it has to come from deep within our heart. Motivated by love. When I first met my wife and started falling in love, I told everyone about her. I never thought about how to say it. I said and did ridiculous things, and everyone forgave me. Why? Because I was crazy in love.

I'm encouraging a natural way of speaking of Jesus. It's not a system or a program—it's real and tailored to you, because it's "Christ in you, the hope of glory" (Colossians 1:27).

10. People DO Want to Talk About Jesus— So Talk About Him

A couple of years ago, a friend and I went to Pearl Street Mall in Boulder, Colorado, with a camera crew. We decided to take a survey, and asked 50 people one question. I had the microphone and people would walk by and I'd say, "Hi, we're taking an independent survey and wondered if you had a second. It's on religion in America and we'd like to know your thoughts on Christianity."

We tried to ask in a casual way. Out of 50 people, how many would you guess were negative about Christianity? Fifty. That surprised me. I thought we might find a few that were part of the club. But the people we asked were really angry. We had to bleep out several words in the documentary. They were all negative about what Christianity represented.

Then we asked 50 people what they thought about the person of Jesus of Nazareth. Out of 50, how many people do you think answered positively? Fifty. All 50 were positive. That amazed me. This survey confirmed that people have an issue with Christianity.

But isn't it a good basis for reconciliation and mutual understanding to start where people are? What if the message of reconciliation that all of us can agree on is actually a person—not a text, theology, doctrine, church, or religion? What if Christianity doesn't own Jesus? What if Jesus is bigger than our religion? That's disconcerting if we're used to being in a comfortable box. What if Jesus acts God-like, going wherever he wants and taking people out of their boxes? What if he gives grace to sinners? What if he moves through people like me to talk to people in scary terrorist-connected groups like Hezbollah and Hamas about Jesus?

If I introduce myself to people as Carl the Christian, the conversation is pretty much over. I can't build a real relationship or real bridge. So I simply tell people I'm a guy named Carl and I would like to be friends, and I've been trying to follow a person named Jesus. I don't even say I'm a follower of Jesus, because that seems too presumptuous, so I say I'm trying to follow Jesus.

I actually said this to a leader in Baghdad: "We think Jesus is here because 2,000 years ago, Jesus was always in the place where the religious leaders thought he shouldn't be." Isn't that true? He was always with the "wrong" people at the "wrong" time. As Christians, we're tempted to think Jesus is ours and we have him all sealed up in a box. Then we're frustrated when people allow him out of the box.

In my experience, sharing Jesus is not all that difficult, even in a hostile environment. I don't tell people that they're sinning and that they're going to go to hell unless they believe what I believe. I just speak of Jesus.

I'm telling you this because I know how powerful and dynamic Jesus becomes when unleashed to live his life at the center of ours. Keep moving further and further into this way of thinking until you're free to speak of Jesus often and always.

#sharejesus:

I don't tell people that they're sinning and that they're going to go to hell unless they believe what I believe. I just speak of Jesus.

11. Point People to Jesus

A few years ago, I was the interim pastor of a church in Colorado Springs, and I studied and prepared my weekly sermons at Poor Richard's, a little coffee shop/restaurant/used bookstore downtown. I had heard it was the toughest place in town. It's where all the gays, Wiccans, and generally odd people hung out. So I thought, "Perfect, sounds like a place Jesus would be, so I'll go study there."

One day I struck up a conversation with Ed, the bookstore manager. I think I was buying a couple of old Philip Yancey books (Christian-type books were always really cheap there). As Ed looked at my books and then looked at me (we had not talked before), I asked, "So, what do you think about Christians?"

It was hilarious. I'll never forget the look on his face as he tried to be nice to his customer in front of him. "Uh. Yeah. Good. No problem," he muttered, looking a bit sheepish.

I pressed him. "Come on, tell me the truth."

"Well, there was that one time that they threw a brick through our window. And when they talk bad about us on the radio. And when they preach against us outside. And..."

It was like the dam broke when he knew that I really wanted to hear. When he paused, I said, "Where do you think Jesus would be if he were here in Colorado Springs right now?"

"Focus on the Family?" he replied with a questioning tone, obviously unsure he was qualified to answer such a question.

I slapped the countertop he was standing behind and made a buzzer sound and said, "Nope. Wrong answer. You know where Jesus would be, Ed? Right here at Poor Richard's. And I'm trying to follow him, so I try to come where he'd be."

I went on to ask if he'd ever noticed me reading the Bible in the corner. Ed said he had and was surprised, but didn't want to ask about it. I told him I prepared my talks there every week for the church I preached in on Sundays. He was so confused.

Then I asked him my favorite question. I said, "Ed, if Jesus came into this room right now—I mean, physically was here— who do you think he'd prefer to go hang out with, me or you?" Like everyone else I ask, he got the answer wrong. He said it would be me. I hit the counter again and made that buzzer sound and said, "Ed, you're not doing well. You're zero for two. Jesus would for sure go home with you. You need to read the book, bro."

"What book?"

"The Bible. The book about Jesus. It's all in there. He was always making religious people angry—the ones who thought they owned him and all truth. Because he kept hanging out with people they thought were inappropriate. The sinners. Lepers. Prostitutes. Samaritans. Ed, he would choose you."

I felt moved as I saw his response to this shocking assertion, so I walked around the counter and put my hand on Ed's shoulder. I said, "Ed, Jesus is for you. He is not against you. He actually likes you. It's my type, the religious ones, who need to be careful lest we find ourselves on the very opposite side of Jesus."

He nearly began to cry. He then asked me if I was a Christian because he'd never heard a Christian say anything like this before. I explained that "being Christian" wasn't the point, but that I was actually trying to follow Jesus.

The distance between people and Jesus isn't doctrinal. It isn't political or social or even theological. It's a matter of personal contact. My job—no, my joy—comes from sharing the good news of Jesus with people. I point to him, and he does all the heavy lifting. I don't have to convince anybody of anything. I let Jesus run his kingdom.

#sharejesus:

Jesus is for you. He is not against you. He actually likes you.

12. Be *for* Something, Not Just *Against* Things

For some unknown reason, Christians are known almost universally known as the people who are "against things." As I've already mentioned, I used to live in Colorado Springs, a city divided politically and socially. Battle lines were drawn on both sides of almost every issue imaginable. My friend Phillip describes it as "Briargate vs. Downtown: a home game where all the players get injured and nobody wins."

The Briargate area of town is, for the most part, the bastion of conservative evangelical Christianity, home turf for some pretty big ministries and nonprofit organizations. The downtown area, on the other hand, is a haven for the gay and lesbian crowd, for the tattooed, the pierced, the outcasts, and the revolutionaries. It's the home turf for a lot of the liberals.

As a result, there's always a rally or a picket line somewhere in town. Feelings are pretty heated about current issues, and sometimes the name-calling and the mudslinging reach newsworthy status. For many conservative Christians, the arguments are about social policy, political activism, and countering the so-called liberal agenda of the homosexuals, the abortion-rights people, and sometimes just about anybody else who believes differently. For liberals, there are protests and rallies to undermine or out-shout the "Christian conservatives."

I lived for many years in Beirut, Lebanon, which seems like the place where conflict was invented. So when I got back to Colorado Springs, my first inclination was to find conflict and have a cup of coffee in the middle of it. Conflict is universal in one sense—

people straining to "get them before they get us." One day I took a notebook and went downtown to Poor Richard's. The owner, Richard Skorman, is now a very dear friend of mine. He's on the city council and, among other things, is the local champion and go-to guy for gay-rights issues. He's not a conservative Christian. There were dozens of coffee shops I could go to just in my own neighborhood, but for some reason, I liked it better down at Poor Richard's, even though it was a half-hour drive from my house.

Anyhow, I went that day, took a notebook, and started polling every person I could. I wanted to test out some word associations. I worked for a couple of hours, and I got some surprising results. The most striking responses I got were the replies to questions like "What do Christians do?"

Eighty-five percent of the people I polled said the same thing, each in different words: "Christians are against things. They fight us and judge us and they hate us."

That should set us all back on our heels.

Guess what Jesus was never accused of? Being against things. He wasn't defined by his hatred of things. Imagine if he were...

"Here comes Jesus, the sin-hater."

"Jesus, Son of David, opposer of liberals, have mercy on me, a sinful man!"

Or the time Jesus asked the disciples, "Who do the people say that I am?" What would they have said?

"Easy, Jesus." Peter raised his hand. "You're against the Romans, the Samaritans, the barbarians, and the French!"

Defining somebody by their opposition would be like labeling a football team by their rivalries. "Featured tonight, on Monday Night Football: the team that trumped the Titans, smashed the Steelers, foiled the Falcons, junked the Jets, and grounded the Giants!"

When we speak of Jesus to friends and people we meet, we focus on what we're for—Jesus—not what we're against.

#sharejesus:

Guess what Jesus was never accused of? Being against things. He wasn't defined by his hatred of things.

13. Choose Friendship Over Manipulation

Just this week I was chatting with a Jewish businessman who said: "I do believe in God. But I just can't believe that only the ones who believe in Jesus Christ are going to heaven." Wow, what a perfect opportunity to talk about his "need" for a Savior. The cross. Justification by faith in Christ alone. Redemption. And all good stuff it is. All good news. But do you think this American Jew was ready to hear that? Don't you think he's heard that a lot throughout his life?

Here's what I said: "Hmm. Interesting. How many children do you have?"

He and his wife, who had just walked in, lit up. They had two. They talked about them for a while and then the man circled back around and said, "Hey, wait a minute. Why didn't you answer me when I said that I don't think you need to believe in Jesus? Aren't you a Christian?"

"Oh," I replied, "I'd just rather talk about your kids than try to convince you of something I believe."

"How refreshing," his wife chimed in. "But you didn't answer my husband. Are you a Christian?"

Again, being careful to answer the real question rather than the stated one, I replied, "I grew up in a Christian home. My religious heritage is Christian, yes. But I am a follower of Jesus."

"What's that?" they both questioned.

I went on to explain what I meant. That I preferred that label over "Christian." They were amazed. Enthralled. We talked about that point for 30 minutes and at the end of our time—it was late at night—they both said: "We've never heard this before. Can we talk more?"

Now, for sure, they had both previously heard the "gospel" from well-meaning Christians trying to convert them. They told me so. Why had it not "worked" before? Possibly because the Christians had led with important truths and religious explanations rather than listening first.

Giving someone a formula or progression to find salvation in Jesus is not a bad thing; it's just ineffective. "All things are lawful for me, but not all things are helpful" (1 Corinthians 6:12, NKJV). If we aren't careful, our "standard ways" of convincing people to follow Jesus can feel like manipulation or an unhealthy focus on something other than, well, actually caring about people!

#sharejesus:

Why doesn't sharing the "gospel" work? Maybe it's because we lead with important truths and religious explanations rather than listening first.

14. Believe in People Like Jesus Believes in People

Jesus believes in people, in unity, and in community. Jesus believes in the power of uniting people in spite of, or perhaps because of, their differences.

Authors Philip Yancey and Dallas Willard have each gone to great lengths to explore the diversity of Jesus' friendships and the way he related to people of different varieties. In their books—which I recommend to any student of Jesus—they uncover the genius of Jesus weaving together a tapestry of diversity. The band of brothers who followed Jesus consisted of people with—get this—*different religious beliefs.* Different sects, and groups that hated and feared each other. Jesus believed in the power people could wield when they converged on a common goal, a common relationship.

The importance of relationship was clear immediately after Jesus' execution. The disciples holed themselves up, not to plan a new game strategy or formulate a way to continue the kingdom without a king, but to mourn, fear, and grieve their confusion and loss. Jesus was their common thread. He was the one they all agreed on, with the notable exception of Judas (now dead), and the possible exception of Thomas, who was so shaken that Jesus later had to prove himself to Thomas to lift his shattered hope from the ashes.

The way of Jesus promotes the power of the heart over the power of the brain. Jesus believed that his followers could converge with passion—that they could come together by what was in their hearts, which would lead to changed minds. Jesus still believes this, if it is indeed true that he never changes. Jesus cares about reaching hearts—wounded, broken, crazy, stubborn, and radical hearts. Different heartbeats, different pains, but the same longing to be loved.

Jesus believes that faith did not arise from logical deduction, but from need, from pain, from hopelessness. Jesus' way was and is the way of the heart.

#sharejesus:

The way of Jesus promotes the power of the heart over the power of the brain.

15. Remember: The Message of Jesus Is *Good* News!

Remember that, for the most part, the people around Jesus loved him. They tried to make him king several times. Even by force. He started preaching the Sermon on the Mount with his immediate disciples listening, and by the end crowds had gathered. His audiences frequently numbered 4,000 or 5,000 people. Amazing, since there was no advertising in his day. No TV or radio to announce the location of his next campaign. No one knew where he would be holding his next meeting unless they were already following him, or at least close by.

Who wouldn't like this man? Think about what he did. He healed the sick. Cast out demons from the demonized. Fed the hungry and the poor. Loved sinners. Honored children and women. And was hard on the establishment. Luke tells us in Acts that Jesus of Nazareth "went around doing good" (Acts 10:38). People tend to like guys like this.

Are you familiar with the mission statement of Jesus?

"The Spirit of the Lord is on me, because he has anointed me to preach good news to the poor. He has sent me to proclaim freedom for the prisoners and recovery of sight for the blind, to release the oppressed, to proclaim the year of the Lord's favor" (Luke 4:18-19).

It's fascinating that when Jesus quotes this passage, which comes from Isaiah 61, he omits one part. In the original version Isaiah continues with "and the day of vengeance of our God" (Isaiah 61:2). Why didn't Jesus say that part? I believe it's because it doesn't fit—at the time anyway—with the good part of the good news he wants to proclaim.

For those who are desperate, Jesus is always good news. He's the one who's rescuing them. Saving them. But Jesus is a constant threat to the establishment—religious or political.

Here's the bottom line: Most of the time, when we share about the life Jesus is offering us, it's all good news. If it's not, let's make sure we're doing whatever we can to remove the obstacles so others can hear it.

#sharejesus:

For those who are desperate, Jesus is always good news. He's the one who's rescuing them.

16. Respect Other People

A few years ago, I experienced a slightly humorous and possibly profound illustration of how we can focus on Jesus rather than on our "Christianity." I accepted an invitation to participate in a citywide discussion, hosted by a church, on the topic of interfaith dialogue. The church had already invited the local Catholic bishop, the leader of the local mosque and Islamic center, and two Jewish rabbis. They needed one more Muslim leader and one more Christian.

The more complicated question was whether or not I'd represent "Christianity," given my propensity to focus on Jesus and leave the religious stuff to others. But the organizers knew me a bit and said it was okay if I just talked about Jesus and didn't worry about explaining or defending the doctrines of Christianity. So I agreed.

Each of us was supposed to answer two questions, and we each had three to five minutes to respond. The first question was "How does your religion get you to heaven?"

Good question!

When my turn rolled around, I was praying for wisdom and something significant to say. This is what came out: "Actually, my religion doesn't get you to heaven."

I probably should have explained or added to that, but that's all I said. The other panelists shifted uncomfortably in their seats and the host asked if I'd like to explain a little more.

"Sure," I said. "It's just that I've never seen a religion save anyone. All religions are great at laying out some basic rules—do's and don'ts—that are good for our lives, but they don't really provide hope or any kind of eternal security. Religions end up causing more trouble than solving anything."

"So then," asked the host, "how do you get to heaven?"

This all seemed so basic, but I thought I might as well go ahead and state the obvious. "Well, it's Jesus. He didn't start a new religion. He came to provide us a model for life and a way to God. He's it. Believing in and following him is the way. He takes us to heaven, not a religion."

On to simple question number two.

"How does your religion deal with terrorism?"

Here's what I said when they got to me:

"I don't really know. I'm not sure how the religion I grew up in would or should deal with terrorism. But I do have some thoughts about how Jesus might deal with terrorists because he had two with him in his inner circle of friends: a Zealot and a tax-collector. A political insurgent and an economic terrorizer of the common folk. What he did with these two was bring them in as confidants. As students. Disciples. And he made them apostles of the early faith. It actually seems to me that the worse someone was, the more Jesus liked him or her. He didn't just have 'mercy' in the way we think of it, as a sweet, sappy, lovey-dovey sort of thing. It was mercy with a bite. Mercy that led the people out of where they were into a new place. This is what Jesus did with the worst people of his day. He was really only hard on one type of folks: people like us."

I looked down the line and smiled. "People like me. Hypocrites and such."

I'm sure at this point they were all wondering why I'd been invited. We did questions and answers for about 20 more minutes and then wrapped it up. Two things happened at the end of the night that made it all worthwhile. I had a little crowd of people around me asking questions. Some happy, others angry, and still others just slightly confused. One woman was more than a little upset with me. I'd obviously shaken up the box where she kept her faith and she needed to tell me a few things. Our conversation went something like this:

"You didn't even mention the Trinity!" she said.

"True," I replied, "but I didn't think I was talking about that, and it didn't come up in the course of the conversation, so…"

That clearly wasn't good enough.

"But surely you do believe in the Trinity, don't you? And there are some other things you didn't mention as well that you should have, like the atonement."

I knew I needed to tread lightly with her. So I simply said, "You're probably right, and of course I believe everything that's in this book." I held up my Bible, showing her that it appeared well read.

Right then, a young man, hardly able to contain himself, blurted out, "I'm a Muslim. I came with the imam tonight. I'm from his mosque and he invited me to come." He turned and addressed the woman who had been speaking with me and said, "If this man had talked about theology or doctrine or even Christianity, I wouldn't have been interested. I've heard all of that from my Christian friends. But he talked about Jesus in a way I've never heard before and had never thought of. I thought it was amazing."

You cannot force-feed another person your perspective and expect it to stay down. As somebody once told me, "You have to realize every person is an 'I.' " There are only people like you and me. People with full brains and empty hearts. People who need Jesus, not a massive array of doctrine, polemics, and theology lessons. People who need a relationship. People who need to belong before they can believe.

#sharejesus:

You cannot force-feed another person your perspective and expect it to stay down.

17. Don't Live Life With a Circle

Draw a circle on a sheet of paper. Or breathe on the mirror and make a circle in the fog. Inside the circle, make little dots and give them names. These dots represent the people whom you consider solid Christians. Maybe you're one of them. On the outside of the circle, make some other dots. These dots are the ones whom you know are not solid Christians. Maybe they drink/smoke/cuss or even kick their dogs. This circle diagram represents the idea of salvation many of us have. We live in the circle and, to bring others inside of it, we have to convince them to adopt our beliefs. We typically use the word *confession* to describe a change of heart.

So we pick up our metaphorical megaphones to tell the people outside of the circle about God. Some of them are interested. And some of them are not.

But when we stand inside the circle, trying to get people "into the kingdom," we mistakenly do two things wrong. First, we try to "download" the right definitions, doctrines, and beliefs into the brains of people who don't know the Apostle Peter from Homer Simpson. By doing that, we communicate that having the right thoughts is the path to salvation. We're telling them that it's the stuff that happens between their ears that matters. When we focus on ideology, we're not touching thirsty hearts. Thirsty people don't want to memorize theology any more than they want to learn a new language.

Second, we're taking God's job out of his very capable hands. When we point at the boundary, we're trying to define it. But if Jesus is lifted up, he draws people to himself. It isn't our job to lose sleep trying to decide if so-and-so is "in" or "out." When we look at Jesus, in the totality of his love and determination, we realize we're not required to make ourselves his followers by force of reason. We realize he came to us in our poverty of mind and heart. It's our job to follow Jesus, refusing to focus on anything else but the crucified and resurrected Jesus.

When we make sharing our faith a war of ideals, we create casualties on both sides of the boundary. Wherever he went, the pained and lost people he met followed him. Jesus' gospel is that *he is* the kingdom of heaven, and following him means we take on an "easy and light" yoke. He's available, and he's compassionate.

#sharejesus:

Jesus' gospel is that *he is* the kingdom of heaven, and following him means we take on an "easy and light" yoke.

18. Live Life With a Dot

The previous reading was about my "circle" exercise. But now, instead of a circle, make a dot somewhere near the middle of this page. This is the Jesus dot. Sprinkle the rest of the page with dots. Find a dot that has the appropriate distance from the Jesus dot and put your name above it. Find another dot, a dot really close to the Jesus dot, and name it "Carl Medearis." Just kidding. I wanted to see if you were reading or skimming. Anyway, instead of measuring the distance between you and Jesus, make a little arrow from the dot, and point it toward Jesus. You're following Jesus. Find another dot, somebody you know who is trying to follow Jesus, too. Make another little arrow. Continue.

As you go, you'll notice a pattern of attraction. Instead of a theologically manufactured, doctrinally approved boundary, there is only the space between the person and Jesus. The differential is the arrow, which designates the intention of the heart. As Jesus himself pointed out, this arrow is often guided by bare need. "Sinners" are often aware of this need, and the arrow points accordingly. It's interesting to note that morally "superior" people often lack the arrow of those who are much more sinful and much more needy.

Let's take a different approach. Jesus, as a person, is interesting to many—and I don't mean solely as an object of abstract scrutiny. Now, some of the dots may not know Jesus or care to. Maybe their arrows point away from him. Maybe you know a serious Hindu or a committed Buddhist. Their arrow may not point at Jesus, but obviously the little dot is seeking something, looking for some meaning, so you could draw a little squiggly, ambiguously pointed arrow.

When you're done with the sheet, step back and stare at it. Whoa— it's a bit scary, isn't it? There's no line! There's no line telling you whether you are in or out. Maybe your hyper-religious friend is ahead of you! Maybe I'm not as close as you are!

I admit the arrow approach is a massive paradigm shift. Maybe on Sunday you feel close to the Jesus dot. Monday might be different. What to do?

What I'm proposing is simply following Jesus. This means learning from him, obeying his teaching, doing what he did. Instead of trying to define the line that separates the saved from the unsaved, we point to Jesus. We simply encourage people to follow Jesus, no matter how far away their dot appears to be.

So go ahead and throw the circle away! It's okay to be a dot without a perceived circle for comfort. Remember, Jesus is the Way, and he started his ministry by saying, "Follow me."

#sharejesus:

I'm proposing that we simply follow Jesus. This means learning from him, obeying his teaching, doing what he did.

19. Look Beyond "Us vs. Them"

What if I told you that an "us vs. them" model of Christianity misses the point? And that when we speak of Jesus from that paradigm, we're not only ineffective, but we'll also lose the game?

Our identity as Team Christian generates many of our challenges when trying to speak of Jesus to our friends and acquaintances in a way they can hear. If they don't see themselves as part of this winning team, they can feel attacked. And even though we're unconscious of it, we remind them daily in various and sometimes not-so-subtle ways that Team Christian is winning.

Many of "them" have been on the receiving end of a well-meaning but poorly thought-through evangelistic attempt. If you want to "feel under attack," just listen to someone claiming that unless you agree with him or her, you will spend the rest of eternity in a place hotter than a Phoenix sidewalk in August. Lots of the other 60 percent of Americans and a growing population around the world have experienced similar sorts of evangelism. If you are told you're wrong enough times, it won't take you long to resort to drastic tactics to ignore or compete with those challenging you.

If you don't feel like you have to evangelize someone away from their team and onto yours, you can speak of Jesus much more freely and, thus, more effectively. When we make sharing our faith a war of ideals, we create casualties on both sides of the boundary. We fight an "us vs. them" campaign that tries to show that our religion, our logic, our reason, and our theology are better than everyone else's. After demolishing their beliefs, we try to rebuild a structure of proprietary mental acknowledgment. Think the right things, and you'll have the magical bar code the scanners of heaven will accept with a beep.

Ever studied the world's major religious groups? In order of size—biggest to smallest—they are Christianity with about 2.3 billion, Islam with about 1.6 billion, Hinduism almost 1 billion, secular/nonreligious/agnostic/atheist about 800 million, Buddhism about

470 million, Chinese traditional about 460 million, indigenous and tribal groups at 270 million, and Jewish at 15 million.[1]

Notice that we're winning. Or maybe losing? There are a few ways to see this. Let's examine the possibilities.

• Possibility #1: Christianity has 2.3 billion followers. That's the most of anyone. We're winning.

• Possibility #2: Christianity has 2.3 billion followers. But the rest of the world is another 4.6 billion—so we're losing, and losing badly.

• Possibility #3: Christianity has 2.3 billion followers. That includes Catholics and Protestants. Anglicans and Baptists. Pentecostals and Mormons. Jehovah's Witnesses and house churches. So how many are "real" Christians? Bible believing? Born again? Jesus following? Who knows? But I do know one source, the World Christian Encyclopedia, that claims an answer. It defines a group called "Great Commission Christians" as those who believe the gospel is for everyone and that everyone should know Jesus. And there are probably fewer than 1 billion of those.[2] Again, we're losing.

As we've seen, it's hard to know where we stand compared with others. Are there a billion of us? Who *is* us? What about all those folks who call themselves Christians in Serbia or Spain—Orthodox and Catholic—who we might not think have a real friendship with Jesus? Hmm.

So Possibility #4 is to not care about religious distinctions at all. Who cares if we're winning? Who cares who "we" are in this context? We know the standard can't simply be having good theology. Even demons have that. Or using the label. Or going to church. Or being born in a Christian country and having the name Matthew, Mark, Luke, or John.

What if we just admitted that religious distinctions are helpful for the Sociology 101 class at college but not much beyond that? Religion can be a helpful tool to get you through life, but maybe it misses the point. It's okay to go to a building called a church on Sunday at 10 a.m. with all your friends and neighbors and family—and do it just because you're a Christian and that's what Christians do on Sunday morning at 10 a.m. I'd say that's fine. Even healthy. And it might be okay to feel part of the team—Team Christian, where we feel we are sometimes winning and sometimes losing. Nothing wrong with it.

Unless it leads you to miss the main point.

The Pharisees were part of Team Judaism. They were pretty good. The whole club thing was going fairly well. They knew and kept the rules. They invited others to join them. They had a clear identity and a clear sense of mission and purpose. They really only missed one thing: Jesus.

Our identity as Team Christian creates challenges for others—if they don't see themselves as part of this winning team, they can feel attacked. It's funny, because we don't often think of ourselves as winning. In fact, we usually think we're the underdogs, the ones losing with all the others against us. So why does everyone else feel exactly the opposite?

The remedy: Stop playing the "our religion can beat up your religion" game. It's the wrong game anyway, and no matter how you add up the score, we're losing.

#sharejesus:

What if we just admitted that religious distinctions are helpful for Sociology 101 at college but not much beyond that?

20. Jesus-Follower or Christian?

Let's think about the words we use to describe ourselves. Like the word *Christian*, which appears only three times in the entire Bible and is so commonly misunderstood today. I know the word *Christian* is so common and so easy to use that it's almost ludicrous to suggest we get rid of it. Even though I'm pretty sure we'll never stop using it entirely, I never refer to myself as a Christian, although I have to use the word occasionally in reference so people will know what I'm talking about.

It's a completely loaded word, and I think it gets in the way of telling people about Jesus.

"Are you religious?"

"Oh, yes, I'm a Christian."

There's nothing in that exchange that says anything about Jesus. Also, it doesn't say one thing that is universally consistent. It means different things to everybody.

To many Americans, the phrase "born-again Christian" means "conservative, right-wing Republican." In the Middle East, a "Christian" is a descendant of the crusaders, or even worse, a militant who kills Muslims. To some Europeans, being a "Christian" means some kind of connection to the Roman Catholic Church—in their minds, that's an organization that's connected to the Spanish Inquisition and selling the forgiveness of sins (indulgences). Or it can mean Protestant, or even the people who burned others at the stake for not being "elect." In the Far East, and in Africa, the word means roughly the same thing as "Western imperialist." And more often than not, anywhere in the world, *Christian* is a political distinction, separating conservative from liberal, Western from Eastern, one militia from another.

I conclude from this that the word *Christian* is not antibiblical, but it isn't helpful in many of our contexts. I tell people that I am a "follower of Jesus" instead, because it says it all in three words, and it's definitely more true to the New Testament than the alternative. Our words matter because they can either become obstacles that either repel people away from us or draw them to us.

#sharejesus:

I tell people that I am a "follower of Jesus" because it's definitely more true to the New Testament than the alternative.

21. Focus on Discipleship, Not Evangelism

Did you know that the word *evangelism* isn't found in the Bible? The Greek word *evangel* literally means "good news." It is used 118 times in the New Testament, and 82 of those times it is in the context of a verbal proclamation. *Preach, proclaim,* and *testify* are the three words most commonly associated with *evangel*. Although the word *evangelism* isn't in the Bible, there is a biblical precedent for it as a concept.

But there is a better phrase, one I think that is more biblical: the commandment *to make disciples.* True, it only appears once, in Matthew 28:19, but it is a significant command, and it was Jesus' final one. Ironically, this verse is used mostly as a call—to evangelism. Ha!

The word *evangelism* is harmful, at least in my opinion, simply because it endorses a flawed concept. Evangelism, as a method, is dangerous because it's something we "do" to other people. Nobody likes to be "done." Remember the last time the guys in white shirts rode their bikes up to you and tried to tell you that you needed to get saved or whatever? Not fun. It actually feels a little violating to have somebody "do it" to you. Icky.

A friend and I were talking the other day, and he asked me, "Why are so many Christians so weak in their faith and their walk?"

"Well," I said, "I think part of the reason is that we tend to promote the evangelism method of spreading Christianity rather than the discipleship model of Jesus. We get people 'in' and then try to go out and get others. After a while, everybody's 'in' and nobody has any idea how to mature in their faith."

Evangelism leads people to believe that it's a job done solely by evangelists. Therefore, very little actual evangelism—or whatever we're going to call it—is ever done. Making disciples, as opposed to evangelism, is a journey of relationship that encompasses support, trial and error, and difficulty. It isn't based on the explanations and doctrines of a religious system. Evangelism leaves hurt people hurt, sinful people sinful, and religious people religious. Discipleship is a journey that requires change, whereas evangelism is just information. Information, in case you didn't know, is pretty poor at producing change by itself.

Discipleship involves a time commitment. If you love someone, you will spend time with him or her, talking about things you love. Evangelism, because it's event-oriented, often has a short half-life.

#sharejesus:

We tend to promote the evangelism method of spreading Christianity rather than the discipleship model of Jesus.

I believe that the gospel and the religion of Christianity can be two different messages. Even opposed on some points. When we preach Christianity, we have to own it. When we preach Jesus, we don't have to own anything. Jesus owns us. We don't have to defend him. We don't even have to explain him. All we have to do is point with our fingers, like the blind man in the book of John, and say: "There is Jesus. All I know is that he touched me, and where I was once blind, now I see."

As Christians, we're faced with a problem difficult to see because it's so obvious. We're aware of Jesus, but we're focused on the ins and outs of Christianity. We're stuck on its requirements and we're defined by its boundaries, caught in an endless struggle to find out where we fit, if we've "arrived" yet, and if we're doing it right.

We struggle with sin, and yet because of the boundaries, we're forced to decide between being honest about our feelings and hiding for fear we'll be judged. In this state, we're not living in the grace of Jesus. We're trying to maintain our membership.

With Christianity, we always wrestle with the question: "Am I good enough?" But Jesus announced that he was present for those who needed him, as a physician for the ill and wounded. Within the church, we often feel the need to conform—to fit all of life's questions and struggles into a system of answers.

We all know how convoluted this becomes on the personal level. As Christians, we learn to take our struggles and "baptize" them with spiritual phrases. The root problems don't go away; they just vanish behind smoke-and-mirrors so we can get on with it. This is like taking aspirin for brain cancer.

My friend Sameer calls himself a Muslim who follows Jesus. It's confusing—you have to get to know him to understand. About five years ago I was talking with him in his house. He said: "Carl, I figured it out. Here's the answer for the Middle East. People come up to this house, and on the house it says 'Christianity: Do not enter.' "

I said, "That's not what the house says."

"Oh yes," he replied, "in the Middle East the house called Christianity has a subtitle and it says: 'Do not enter' and 'Keep out, we are against you.' "

He went on to say, "We have to take those words off the house, because it's actually not the house of Christianity. It's the house of Jesus. So here's my plan. People get close to the house and they're reading 'Christianity.' They're ready to turn away, but we have to grab them and take them and open up the door and say, 'Look! It's Jesus.' And Jesus will invite them in because Jesus loves people. He's not the guy in the way. He *is* the Way."

#sharejesus:

We're aware of Jesus, but focused on the ins and outs of Christianity—stuck on its requirements and defined by its boundaries.

23. Get Real

How am I supposed to explain the Trinity to people without stumbling over myself or sounding ridiculous? "Well," I say with a sigh, "you see, God is like...an egg." Okay, stop. Let's address this in a way that allows us to be authentic.

The thirsty sinner comes and on bended knee says, "God, I'm thirsty."

And sometimes—let's be honest—we give them a drink from a fire hose. Of course we don't intend to confuse, and I'm not trying to make Christians seem like confusing people. We don't intend to be. But the question invariably comes up: "What do I have to believe now?"

What are we supposed to say? I remember trying to explain the word *sacrifice* to a teenage boy at an outreach. He'd asked me about Jesus being a sacrifice, so I attempted to explain the entire history of Levitical sacrifices for sins, because I hoped he would understand the concept of Jesus sacrificing himself for the faults of sinful people. I lost him at the word *altar*.

"Man," he said, "you may as well be speaking Greek to me."

"Actually," I said, "the children of Israel spoke Hebrew."

I could slap my forehead now, just thinking about it. The better way forward for us is to get in touch with what we really believe, and why. Then we ask questions, share our own doubts, and offer what we know is true about Jesus.

#sharejesus:

The better way forward for us is to get in touch with what we really believe, and why.

24. Hanging Out on the Hard Edge

Instead of spending all our time with Team Christian, what if speaking of Jesus leads us into the "dens of iniquity"? To the places where the "bad people" hang out? To be with outcasts? Muslims? Homosexuals? Liberals? (Or conservatives if you're liberal.) Blacks if you're white or—I think you get it.

Imagine this scene from Luke 7. Jesus has accepted the dinner invitation of a Pharisee, which is itself a surprising thing—showing that Jesus would go anywhere. Jesus is now at the table, resting. Getting ready for dinner. Surely there were others present besides Jesus and this one Pharisee.

In walks a woman of the night. The room gasps. The Pharisee is sure that Jesus will know who this woman is and quickly rebuke her and send her on her way. But instead Jesus allows her the unthinkable—her tears wet his feet, she wipes them with her hair, then kisses and anoints them with perfume from her alabaster jar.

Wow. A bit sensual, don't you think? Imagine. First of all, how did she know which one was Jesus? She'd obviously seen him before, maybe out healing the sick or casting out a demon. She seemed to know somehow that she needed him. That she wasn't worthy of him. Her actions spoke of pure humility. Brokenness. Asking for healing and forgiveness as she washed the feet of the One who could offer it.

But imagine it from Jesus' side. Or put yourself in his place. Let's say you're a pastor or a youth worker at the home of a wealthy religious leader who also happens to be one of your primary donors. And in walks a local prostitute who comes right up to you.

What would you do? Would you, in your embarrassment, try to ignore her? Would you quickly explain to the other guests that you do not know her? That you have no idea why she's doing this? Would you push her aside? Stand up and walk away? Turn red?

Because Jesus was pure, in heart and actions, he could simply accept her offering. Jesus went on to forgive the woman's sins and then praise her as an example of faith as the shocked Pharisee looked on.

Jesus gravitated to the people who needed him, and the people who knew they needed him were most often experiencing the hard edge of life. Find your way to the hard edge.

#sharejesus:

Instead of spending all our time with Team Christian, what if Jesus leads us to the places where the "bad people" hang out?

25. Invite Outsiders to Be Insiders

Imagine that I'm standing next to a friend who doesn't know Jesus. And he knows he doesn't know. Maybe he's sort of a rough guy. A tough guy. And he knows he's on the "outside." (It always surprises me how often people categorize themselves as "outsiders.")

I say this: *Imagine if Jesus came down right now and was here, physically standing between you and me. Whom do you think he'd prefer? Whom would he want to hang out with, or go have dinner with?* The person always says "you." They think Jesus would want to hang with me because I'm one of "his guys."

As I did with the clerk in Poor Richard's, I make a loud noise and lower my hand as if I'm hitting the buzzer that says "wrong answer." The answer, of course, is the other way around. I explain that Jesus always seemed to prefer the sinners over the religious people. Even though I don't see myself as a "religious guy," I'd probably still be the one on the receiving end of Jesus' criticism. Maybe I'm the "Pharisee." Or even a hypocrite in the sense that I don't always do what I tell others to do.

But outsiders would always be on the inside with Jesus, as long as they understood their need. Jesus loved the humility of those who understood they needed help. That was the issue with the religious leaders. They didn't know that they needed Jesus. They thought they had it all wrapped up. They had their theology down. Their books memorized. Their actions right. They weren't the bad guys— after all, they were the keepers of the law. They were the good guys. The religious police.

It was just the little detail of missing Jesus. That's all.

So he preferred hanging out with the ones who wanted to be with him. Except on a couple of occasions, the religious leaders felt threatened by Jesus. The sinners invited him in. They didn't know who he was, but they knew he loved and accepted them. That's all they needed.

If Jesus were walking our streets today, where would he be? In our churches? Or behind the school where the "interesting" people hang out? Does this mean we shouldn't hang out at church, but behind the school instead? No, but we do need to be aware of our tendencies. We tend to huddle up with our friends on Team Christian. It's easy. We can live our whole social life under a Christian bubble—youth group on Wednesday night, church on Sunday morning, and small group on Sunday night. All great things—but where's the margin for hanging out with the people Jesus gravitated to? Find that margin, and invite the outsiders… inside.

#sharejesus:

Outsiders would always be on the inside with Jesus, as long as they understood their need.

26. Go Ahead—Be Yourself

Jesus was a natural leader, and his favor with people was so broad that his disciples included all of the extremes of his day: the monk-like Essenes, a government-sanctioned tax collector, and a Zealot, the Jewish revolutionary of the time. This is like having a ministry team composed of a super-religious person, a freedom fighter, and an IRS official. His disciples also included a handful of lower-class fishermen and other blue-collar workers.

Jesus appealed in one way or another to all of them. He was never deceitful, he never pandered to them, and he didn't play favorites. So how did he manage to assemble a team of such diverse individuals?

Because he was genuine. He was masterful. He had keen insight and cared deeply for people. He was, in terms of his humanity, an attractive personality, the upper crust of natural intelligence, and a grassroots-recognized leader. He was the man that other men looked to for sincere answers, for hope.

So relax. Enjoy your friends. Enjoy their company along with the company of Jesus. Point him out freely, without fear or intimidation. You're not responsible to sell him to them. You're simply saying what you've seen. You're not the judge. You're the witness. That means you can talk about what's real in your life, including the real impact Jesus is having on it. And you'll see— people will listen. Not because we're so good, but because Jesus is so compelling!

#sharejesus:

You can talk about what's real in your life, including the real impact Jesus is having on it.

27. But Don't Be a Jerk

I'm constantly surprised by how many of my Christian friends seem to revel in how the good news Jesus brought is so tough. It's hard to understand and follow, they say. The myth is that very few of us will be able to figure it out. It's narrow and difficult—like camels through the eyes of needles. It's not a broad path; it's a very narrow path. And it's offensive.

While these hard words do appear in the Bible, they are both misunderstood and overused. And that sometimes causes people to act like, well, jerks!

I remember sitting inside a coffee shop in downtown Colorado Springs with my wife, Chris, and an Italian friend who was close to God's kingdom. Suddenly we heard a ruckus outside. It was a man with a big wooden cross and a bullhorn. As we tuned in, we heard him targeting those of us inside the coffee shop. "Perverts, gays, and Catholics," he was yelling, "hell awaits you."

My Italian friend was more than a little uncomfortable. He may not have been a pervert or gay, but he definitely grew up Catholic. I couldn't believe what I was hearing as this man with a cross, a Bible, and a bullhorn made a mockery of our faith.

I decided to go outside and confront him. I walked up and said, as kindly as I could, "Brother, I, too, am a Christian, and I'm not sure that what you're doing is the best way to approach things."

With fire in his eyes he quoted (sort of) 1 Corinthians 1:18—he told me the message of the cross was foolishness, and that people would be offended by this stumbling block (he used lots of partial quotes from that chapter of Scripture). All of a sudden, someone ran out of the coffee shop and hauled off and punched the guy right in the mouth. It actually knocked him to the ground. His mouth was bleeding, and everyone around was yelling and pushing—I found myself in the middle of a minor riot.

I was torn. This guy was a jerk, for sure. But he didn't deserve to be punched out like a kid on the playground. I leaned over and picked him up, urging him to just go. He did.But as he walked away, he looked at me and said, "Brother, if you're not being persecuted, then what you're preaching isn't real."

Somehow, it felt to me like this guy had missed the point. Being persecuted is one thing. Being a jerk is something completely different.

#sharejesus:

While hard words about the gospel of Jesus do appear in the Bible, they are both misunderstood and overused.

28. Hear What People Are *Really* Concerned About

It's always important that we're answering the real questions people are asking. Jesus was brilliant at this. When people hear that we're Christians, they're generally wondering if we might try to sign them up for Christianity, and if we think our religion is the only good one. If they ask "Is Jesus the only way?" and we answer "Yes," then we've *really* said yes to their underlying question: "Do I need to join your religion called Christianity that condemns to hell all others who believe differently?"

This is where listening is crucial. If you can hear what people are truly concerned about before you answer, it will save you (and them) from lots of confusing conversation.

If you've agreed with my thesis that it's not about joining a religion but following a person, then you can answer others' underlying questions this way:

"I appreciate the question. It's a real one. I've asked it a lot myself and I know many others around the world struggle with wondering whether or not there is 'only one way.' And I'm pretty sure people—even top theologians from all the world's greatest religions—have been struggling with this question for centuries. So let me clarify—would you say that your question has to do with my theology? What I believe about God? Faith? The Bible? Jesus? All of which I'm happy to talk about. Could be a fun conversation. Or is your question more of a thought about all the other Christians you've met in your life who seemed to know the 'final answer' and liked telling you what that was—and what you should do about it?"

We really do want to clarify what others are really asking—it's not a stalling tactic because the question scares us. Not at all. We need to hear, really hear, what they're asking. Most of the time they don't really know exactly what they're asking, or why. And that's okay.

But let's imagine it's a defensive question based on past hurts, with a little bit of "I wonder what you think about this?" mixed in. Slow down, ask questions, and pay attention to the reality under the surface.

#sharejesus:

If you can hear what people are truly concerned about before you answer, it will save you from lots of confusing conversations.

29. Share What Matters Most

Instead of getting bogged down in lots of rabbit-trail questions about complex theological arguments or popular misconceptions about the Bible, narrow your focus to Jesus. Here are some of the typical things I say when I'm talking with people who don't have a lot of interest in church, and are suspicious about Christians in general, but are open to connecting with me...

"Here's the thing. Jesus is good. He *is* good news. He doesn't just know some good news. He is the good news. Have you ever heard the term 'the gospel'? Probably. It's often defined as something we preach at sinners. But in the Bible Jesus used the word *gospel* as a way to proclaim a new way of living and loving and being loved—it's the good news of Jesus. That's what he does for us—he gives us life. He heals and restores us. He gives us answers to our deepest human questions. And he shines light on the truth, and gives us a way to live forever. These are all good things.

"You've also probably heard the word *repent* and wondered why these gospel preachers are demanding that you repent. Actually the word *repent* just means to turn around and start going in the right direction. When you're lost on the road (not that I would ever be lost, but maybe you have been) then you'd be 'repenting' when you turn around and go the right way. Jesus says we should do that and follow him because it's good for us. It's the right thing to do—not to sign up for a certain religious identity, but to have life. Real and full life. Good news, indeed.

"So is he the only way to that kind of good news for everyone? I think so. But if you find pygmies and Buddhists and Hindus and Muslims and people who call themselves Christians who've somehow found fulfillment outside of Jesus—I'm not going to argue with them. I'm not here to say who's in and who's out. I'm not God. But as far as I can tell, Jesus is the best news around, and everyone I've ever told about him seems to like him. Some even choose to follow him and commit themselves to his way. But it's totally your choice. No pressure from me!

"And please don't ever think that God is up in heaven on his big white throne, with his long gray beard and big iron scepter in his hand just waiting to smack someone who goes awry. That's such a faulty picture of God. Jesus told us the real picture in Luke chapter 15. It's a picture of God running to the kid who has really, really messed up his life—who has turned to come crawling back home. But God can't wait for him, so he runs to the kid and hugs him. Kisses him. Rewards him and welcomes him home. That's the real God. And that's what we and everyone else get when we say yes to Jesus. Good news, man. I'm telling you, it's good news!"

#sharejesus:

Here's the thing. Jesus is good. He is good news. He doesn't just know some good news. He *is* the good news.

30. Talking Is Better Than Debating

Too often I have tried to win allies to my point of view rather than pointing to Jesus. I remember having lots of arguments with people of different perspectives. I exercised my tongue and my brain a lot in those situations. I fervently and (I hope) intelligently refuted arguments. I showed my mettle. I proved myself.

I proved that it was more important to me to win an argument than to be like Jesus—compassionate and loving, kind and patient. Oops.

In the 1920s a missionary named E. Stanley Jones traveled to India to bring the good news of Jesus to the Hindus, the Muslims, and the Buddhists who lived there. He found himself standing in line behind Moses and David, Jesus and Paul, and Western civilization and the Christian church. He wrote: "I was worried. There was no well-defined issue. I found the battle almost invariably being pitched at one of these three places: the Old Testament, or Western Civilization, or the Christian Church. I had the ill-defined but instinctive feeling that the heart of the matter was being left out. Then I saw that I could, and should, shorten my line, that I could take my stand at Christ and before that non-Christian world refuse to know anything save Jesus Christ and him crucified."[3]

Does that sound familiar? It's the same thing the Apostle Paul, in his old age, told the Jesus-followers living in Corinth: "For I resolved to know nothing while I was with you except Jesus Christ and him crucified" (1 Corinthians 2:2).

Jones continues this thought in his book *The Christ of the Indian Road:* "The sheer storm and stress of things had driven me to a place that I could hold. Then I saw that there is where I should have been all the time. I saw that the gospel lies in the person of Jesus, that he himself is the Good News, that my one task was to live and to present him. My task was simplified."[4]

Jones continues: "I found that when I was at the place of Jesus I was every moment upon the vital. Here at this place all the questions in heaven and earth were being settled. He was the one question that settled all others."[5]

When I struggled as a "typical" missionary in Lebanon, failing to convince even a single person to commit to Christianity, the words of E. Stanley Jones struck me with profound and simple truth. The gospel is not a debate or a list of things to believe. The gospel is a person. Jesus Christ is the gospel. He is the truth. He is the point. He embodies all of the salvation/redemption/forgiveness/freedom stuff himself, and because he is a personality, he does not require that I win a debate or argument before he can connect with an individual.

#sharejesus:

The gospel is not a debate or a list of things to believe. The gospel is a person.

31. Be Prepared for All Kinds of Questions

Based on my experience, three-quarters of our opportunities to share our love for Jesus happen accidentally. It's not us taking Jesus to other people; it's them bringing the questions to us. And it's usually not a neutral meeting of the minds.

"Yeah, there's probably a God, but I'm not a fanatic about it—why are you?" Sometimes, following Jesus doesn't seem remotely sensible to others.

Have you ever been deliberately poked regarding your faith? If you're still reading this far into the book, chances are good that at some point or another, somebody decided to prod you about your faith.

It could have been the guy in science class leaning over to say something he knew would offend you, then asking why you're always talking about your community service, then asking you why you go to church when you could be sleeping in. Maybe you have a friend who likes everything about you, but has no interest in that "religious" side of you. The questions and objections are both mildly threatening ("How could anybody believe the world is only 6,000 years old?") to angry ("If God is really loving, then why did he let my mother die?") to passive-aggressive ("That's fine for *some* people who think a certain way, but not for me").

These kinds of questions can put us off—but I think they're actually like invitations. If we can forget about feeling threatened by them, we can unleash our curiosity. Ask lots of questions, and then follow your questions with more questions. Sooner or later, you'll have an opening to say something true and good in the conversation.

#sharejesus:

Three-quarters of our opportunities to share our love for Jesus happen accidentally.

32. Convincing People Isn't Your Job

When we don't feel like we have the burden to convince the world that they're wrong and we're right, then we can talk with total freedom about Jesus and how amazing he was and is. It's not a contest. There is no score—or at least, we don't know what the score is. There are sheep and there are goats, according to Jesus, but we've admitted we sometimes confuse the two. A billy or a ram, a ewe or a nanny—they can all look alike from a distance, and we may not be as good at knowing the difference as we once thought.

What if we didn't worry or think so much about "those people" and simply loved them? To be clear, how about we replace the word *loved* with the phrase *being nice to*? What if we were just really nice to people? And talked about Jesus constantly?

No person, anywhere in the world, has a brain-port open to receive a personality change. There are only people like you and me. People with full brains and empty hearts. People who need Jesus, not a fire hose of Bible facts and arguments. People who need a relationship. People who need to belong before they can believe.

We can only do one of two things: Give them Jesus or give them wasted sewage. We can either point the way to the Way or confuse them with a load of things that will never feed their need for God. There is a place for Bible trivia and science and history and apologetics, but these things are not Jesus—they are humanly manufactured attempts to make people think that having the right ideas is the same thing as loving and following Jesus.

And ultimately, you and I cannot change another person. That's Jesus' job, not ours.

#sharejesus:

What if we didn't worry or think so much about "those people" and simply loved them?

33. Seize the Crazy Opportunities

One of my favorite things to do is to invite Jesus into meal conversations. Once a friend of mine, a doctor in Beirut, decided to host an expensive dinner at an upscale restaurant in the city. He invited Chris and me, and of course we attended. I found out afterward that the meal cost him well in excess of $3,000.

During the meal, we attracted the attention of a member of Parliament who was also dining at the restaurant. After some time, he and his entire entourage came over and joined us. After they sat down there were about 30 people packed around the table. Everybody was having a great time. My doctor friend rose to his feet and said that we ought to go around the table, one at a time, each with a minute to say something.

Great. As it happened, I was the third person in line. So I got to my feet, toasted the doctor, and thanked him for the meal. I said that I was extremely grateful for the chance to live in their community, that they had taught me so much about Jesus, and that Jesus had become the most important thing to me in the whole world.

What happened next rated a flat-out 10 on my funny meter. For some reason, without exception, every person after me felt obligated to say something about Jesus. Chris and I were the only people at the table who weren't Muslims, and here, in this dining room late at night in Beirut, 30 Muslims were standing and saying openly gracious stuff about Jesus. I don't know if it was peer pressure or not, but it was the highlight of my week. I was in stitches all the way home.

Chris thought it was funny, too. "Have you ever seen anything like that?" she laughed.

"No, I haven't," I said, "but if Jesus keeps that up, we're going to need a new job in no time."

"Yeah, right," she said.

What's really intriguing to me is how simple it is to share Jesus with other people as opposed to trying to make "Christians" out of them. When I was younger and just starting out, I used to ask people, "Do you believe in God?" I would spell out God's plan of salvation and do these ridiculous illustrations to convince people that it was logical to believe in God.

"See, God is like an egg," I would tell them. "There's one egg, but there are three components, and that's like God because…"

I'm certain that every time I did that, one angel would nudge another angel as they looked down from above and say, "Hey, everybody, check this out. Medearis is doing that egg thing again." Oh yeah—I'm telling you, I used to try to explain God's existence. With an egg, no less.

Now I sit in upper-crust restaurants and try not to laugh my head off as my Muslim friends scramble to think of the nicest things they can say about Jesus.

Yes, I'm being funny (or trying to be), but I'm making a point. Jesus is portable. No, it's not as if we're carrying him somewhere. More the other way around. All I do is point to him as he carries me.

#sharejesus:

It's so simple to share Jesus with other people, as opposed to trying to make "Christians" out of them.

34. Lean Into Learning When You're Opposed

When I was younger and still hammering my mind on the anvil of higher education, I had a professor who was a passionate atheist, and he loved to take Christianity to task for any reason. He was good at it, too. In class, we'd discuss the Crusades, the church, the Reformation, and the negative effects of Christianity on the world. He would relentlessly accuse the church of disrupting or destroying native cultures with "Christian" standards. South America, the South Pacific islands, Africa, you name it. He was like an evangelist. He hoped to help the uninformed Christians find the light. It was intense, but it was one of my formative seasons of my life. It actually began to shape in my mind what was wrong with Christendom.

There'd be 50 students in his world history class, and easily half of us considered ourselves some type of Christian. We were prime targets. A strange ritual would begin: The room would almost physically change temperature. The air would thicken. The silence between declarations would speak with thunderous intensity. The professor would posture, pose questions, deliberate, and then level some withering conclusion at the establishment of Christianity. Christians. Us!

We would nudge each other and give sideways glances that asked, *Why don't you say something?*

What exactly were we supposed to say?

These moments are painful because they make us look inside. By causing us to look at ourselves, we wrestle with self-doubt, which in turn can make us discouraged. We look at the real condition of our lives; we briefly examine our satisfaction with Christianity, wonder why we're still struggling, and ask: *Why am I so sure, and, if I am so sure, I should easily be able to share with somebody else, right? What do I really believe? What is my faith? What is the message I believe—what is the gospel?*

As uncomfortable as all of this is, these are fantastic questions to chew on. They help you develop honest answers to honest questions. And you'll need those honest answers as you tell people about your love for Jesus.

#sharejesus:

By causing us to look at ourselves, we wrestle with self-doubt, which in turn can make us discouraged. But this actually helps us.

35. Avoid the Defensiveness Trap

The Western church is attempting to legislate morality in order to maintain a society that is pure, safe, and peaceful—which, in and of itself, is not a bad desire. But when we're injured by the pushback we encounter, we get defensive. Under fire from a hostile and misunderstanding world, we grow hostile ourselves—we challenge and scoff at the people who oppose us, and demolish the character and teachings of people in popular culture.

It's difficult to "love the sinner and hate the sin" when we adopt a defensive posture. I think it's a huge mistake to turn morality into a politically, legally enforced code, because doing so creates more division and defensive posturing. Have you ever noticed how quickly a fight or debate turns against you when you become defensive?

"What's wrong?" my wife asked me one evening when I got home.

I slumped against the wall by the door, and waited a minute before answering her. "Nothing," I said. "Nothing, huh?" She was drying her hands with a dishtowel, looking at me suspiciously.

"Yep," I said shortly. I kicked off my shoes, went to the bathroom, and rinsed my face. Oh, what a day. I dried off, went out to the living room, and sat down on the corner of the couch.

"We the jury," Chris said as she came in and sat down on the couch opposite me, "find you guilty of fibbing. Something's wrong—out with it."

I don't like being pressed, even if I am guilty of fibbing. "Nothing's wrong," I barked at her, "so quit bugging me, okay? Is that all right with you, huh?"

I went to the bedroom and fell backward on the bed. I stared at the ceiling.

Busted. Pure and simple.

Chris stood in the doorway with a small smile on her face. "Care to make a statement before I take you down to the station for questioning?"

I had to laugh. It was a small argument, less than five minutes in duration, yet it proved an irrefutable point, a lesson I constantly seem to be learning. As soon as you get defensive, you prove your own guilt.

And so it is with Christendom. When you fill your mind with all of the explanations, you are prepping for a fight whether you want one or not. Because, believe it or not, there are millions of people who totally disagree with you. They may even think you're an idiot, wasting your life on something you can't see, hear, feel, touch, or taste. Instead of prepping your arguments, remind yourself to listen to Jesus. He told his disciples it would be better for them if he left, because his Spirit would come to live in their hearts, teaching them everything they needed to know about him. We have that Spirit in us, willing and able to help us engage a disbelieving world. Let's depend on him, instead of our arguments.

#sharejesus:

As soon as you get defensive, you prove your own guilt.

36. Respond With Love—Always

One day my friend Richard stunned me with a surprise phone call. Here's how the conversation went down.

"Carl—it's Richard. You have a minute?"

"Yep, go ahead." I poured myself a cup of coffee and settled down in the chair by my front window.

"Patricia and I are going to have some of our friends over to observe and celebrate the Passover, and we'd like to invite you and Chris to join us."

Okay, my turn to be confused. I hadn't thought of Richard and Patricia as religious in any way, but I was instantly intrigued. "Of course," I said, "we'd be honored. When and where?"

He gave me the details, and I hung up the phone. I couldn't wait to tell Chris—she'd love it.

The meal was kosher, and it was superb—Richard is an excellent chef. The company was as diverse as it could get. It seemed Chris and I were the only guests who weren't tattooed or pierced or gay. At some point in the meal we passed around a tray with crackers, and each person took a moment to stand and say something. Without exception, every single guest made some statement or another about being grateful for freedom. I could only assume most of them were talking about being free to express their beliefs or being gay. A few of them even said so. Finally, it was my turn.

Well, what does Carl do when somebody gives him the floor? He talks about Jesus, even if it is a Passover celebration, even if none of the people next to him want to hear it.

Okay, so it was a little un-kosher, but I talked about my gratitude that Jesus was in my life and how Chris and I had come to believe that following Jesus was the ultimate freedom. There was a pause as I sat down. Chris stood and shared next. I sat there with my jaw hanging down to my belt buckle—she was stunning, talking about how she discovered that Jesus is the most important friend we have, and how much she loved him.

After the meal, a young woman approached us. She started crying as soon as she opened her mouth to speak. "Listen." She took hold of my arm and looked up at me. "I used to be one of them, you know."

"One of who?" I asked.

"You people. I used to be born again. A Christian."

"Really?" I asked. "I wouldn't have guessed, but uh, tell me what happened."

She started to shake, sobbing louder. "I'm a lesbian," she said. "I fought it every step of the way, too. Finally, I couldn't take it anymore. I was drowning in guilt and shame, and I was so afraid that if I told anybody about my struggle, they wouldn't understand; they wouldn't want to ever see me again."

"And?" Chris asked. I looked at her, and we both knew what was coming.

"I finally told my pastor, I asked him if there was anything he could do to help me, if there was some counselor or something. I was so desperate. I thought there was something wrong with me, and I thought it was going to kill me." She stopped crying and looked at us. Her face was pinched and sorrowful. "He told me to get out, to not come back. He said there was no place for me in the kingdom of God. He said that God hates people like me."

"I'm so sorry," was all I could say.

"Do you believe that?" Chris asked her. "I...I don't know," she answered.

"What about Jesus?" I asked. "What do you feel about Jesus?"

"I've always tried to love Jesus, and I've always wanted him," she said, simply.

"Well, it sounds to me like you have the main thing right," I said, "and maybe your struggle with your lifestyle is secondary."

"You think so?" she asked.

"Yes, I do."

"What's your position on gays?" she asked.

I didn't even have to think about that one. "The same as Jesus'—to love them."

"Do you think there's something wrong with being gay?"

I paused for a moment—I had to think. "I have a tendency to lust," I said. "Is there something wrong with that?"

"Well of course," she said, "it's a sin."

"Does that mean that it's okay to lust?"

"No," she said, "but it doesn't mean that Jesus doesn't want to save you."

"Exactly," I said. "My faults don't keep Jesus from me, but they can keep me from him."

"What are you saying?" she asked.

"That I don't have to change for Jesus to love me. But I do have to change if I am going to love him back."

"You mean that your sin is no different from my sin?" she asked. "There is no difference—sin is sin. It keeps all of us from Jesus, to the point where we prefer our way to his way."

When we respond with love to people, then love will help us find our way through difficult conversations.

#sharejesus:

There is no difference—sin is sin. It keeps all of us from Jesus, to the point where we prefer our way to his way.

37. Reconsider What It Means for Someone to "Convert"

We recently hosted a summertime gathering of some of our longtime friends from the Middle East and brought in a bunch of American Christian friends to talk about God, the Middle East, and how to bring hope to Muslim countries. There were about 45 of us together here in Colorado for three days. We were having a great time—until I looked over and saw two of our guests all tangled up.

The next thing I knew, my Muslim friend (not yet a follower of Jesus) had gone out on the deck and was smoking a cigarette like his life depended on how fast he could suck it down. I walked out and nonchalantly said, "What's up, bro?"

His response: "Why the $%&^@ do these people want to convert me? Why can't they just leave me alone? I know that you don't want to convert me. Right?"

Talk about a loaded question. Here's my answer, and what happened...

I asked him what he thought my other friend wanted to convert him to. He said, "He wants me to be a Christian, but I'm a Muslim." I asked him what he thought this friend meant by becoming a Christian.

"He wants me to stop living in the Middle East and loving my family." I told him I was pretty sure that's not what this friend meant, but if that's what "conversion to Christianity" is, then I agreed—he shouldn't convert.

"See," he said to me, "I knew you weren't into conversion."

"No, I'm not," I said. "Not like that. Not at all. I think you should stay in your country, love your family, and be who God has made you to be." Then I asked him this: "What do you think God thinks when he looks down at all nearly 7 billion people on earth?" "He thinks they're all messed up," he said.

"Yep, that's what I think God's thinking, too. So what do you think God would like to do with all these messed-up people? Muslims, Christians, Jews, Hindus, nothings, everyone?"

He had never thought of that before, so he wasn't sure. But he did say God would probably want to "help them not be so messed up." I agreed.

"So you might say that God would like to convert all nearly 7 billion people on earth. Not to a religion, but to himself. He would like everyone to be like him. To be converted into him. But how would he do that? He'd need a converter."

I went on to tell my friend that if he bought an appliance here in the United States and took it back to the Middle East, he'd need something to change the current from 110 to 220 volts. "What's that called?" I asked him.

"A transformer or converter," he said.

"That's right. So what is God's transformer to get us all back the way God wants us to be? To change us? To convert us?"

He gasped (literally) and said, "It's Jesus. I never thought of that—but it's Jesus. He's the converter."

He got so excited he called his wife out and told her the whole conversation. She started to cry. We sat on the deck and prayed that God's "converter" or "transformer" would change us into the current that can be connected to God. And that he would do this with all of our friends.

The language we typically use to engage others about the things that matter most in life is frequently misunderstood and even offensive-sounding to others. We must get past the lazy language we use and find ways to communicate the heart of our heart. The key to that is embedded in my conversation with my Muslim friend: Always connect back to our own reality, and to the heart of God as revealed in Jesus.

#sharejesus:

The language we typically use to engage others about the things that matter most in life is frequently misunderstood.

38. Practice the Art of Humility

Jesus' way was a way of humility, a lifestyle of service without self-exaltation. It was the way of foot-washing, the way of meekness, the way of preferring others, of living for the glorification of something bigger. Jesus' way was the way of big dreams. When Jesus initially sent out his disciples, he gave them a task that was much, much bigger than anything they could accomplish on their own.

Jesus' way required big faith. He knew that giving his friends an unimaginably huge task would require their reliance on him and inspire their passions, fanning them into a bonfire that would last long after he was gone.

Let's not make it hard to hear and receive this wonderful message of Jesus and his kingdom by our own shortcomings. Jesus loved the humility of those who understood they needed help.

I often think that Paul reflects a kind of success that we in the West can relate to because we want so badly to succeed. This is ironic because, as time went on, Paul began to refer to himself more negatively. He went from calling himself an apostle to calling himself the very worst sinner ever. It's almost like he discovered more and more each day that his contribution to the world was insignificant. And yet in his core he realized that Jesus' contribution was more than enough. He understood what his role was—and what it wasn't. When we engage others about Jesus or faith or the big questions in life, do we enter into the conversation and fuel it with the kind of humble self-knowledge that invites them to go deeper?

#sharejesus:

Let's not make it hard to hear and receive this wonderful message of Jesus and his kingdom by our own shortcomings.

39. Be Perfect (Just Kidding!)

Paul once wrote, "When I came to you, brothers, I did not come with eloquence or superior wisdom as I proclaimed to you the testimony about God. For I resolved to know nothing while I was with you except Jesus Christ and him crucified. I came to you in weakness and fear, and with much trembling" (1 Corinthians 2:1-3).

As that phrase about fear and trembling crossed my mind, I found I could easily relate to Paul. I found the "decision" to be weak less voluntary. I trembled because, on many occasions as a missionary in the Middle East, there were murderers breathing the same air as *moi*. And one of my chief concerns was keeping Mrs. Medearis' husband in good health.

Most of the time people are looking for answers, and even the angry individuals are, in a sense, pleading. The plea is unique— more helplessness than cynicism. Sometimes it's a blunt statement, coming without pretext or warning. A desperate friend, a depressed acquaintance in a rare moment of honesty. Maybe even a complete stranger. But whoever they are, for whatever reason, they say, "My life stinks." Or something like that.

We think, *Your life stinks? How can you say it with such candor? So honestly? Is it desperation?*

Is it our obvious virtues (ha!) that encourage these people to share, or just freak circumstances? We panic, we fumble, we falter, and we blurt out something weak. Or worse, anecdotal. Or we realize we don't have a clue what to say. The problem posed to so many of us is the blatant reality of Jesus' good news itself. What is that good news, how do we live it, and what do we share?

What's so discouraging about sharing your faith is that you tend to come away from it less sure than you went in. Did I share everything I should? What did I miss? What if the person only heard a part of it and joins a weird cult?

The nausea, the sweaty palms, the dizzy spells, the sweat dripping down your sides—ah yes. I call it a tender spot. During many occasions, I've done everything from freezing in the headlights to playing it cool. And all because I was never really sure what to say. Mostly, I had the wrong message. I felt I needed to clarify Christianity, answer for the Crusades, solve the problem of Original Sin, and defend the history of the church. What a weight!

Let's make this simple—find the questions people are most interested in pursuing, then get to the heart of those questions as you're talking with them. When you get to the heart of their question, share what's at the core of your own heart—your love for Jesus.

#sharejesus:

Most of the time people are looking for answers, and even the angry individuals are, in a sense, pleading.

40. A (Super-Short) History of Christianity

When I speak at different universities, one of my favorite things to do is to ask the students if they think I can give the history of Christianity in 20 minutes or less. Invariably, almost everybody thinks I can't. So I have somebody start a stopwatch, and I attempt to give the class the whole thing—all 2,000 years of it—before the timer buzzes. Now, admittedly, this 20-minute condensed version is very Western and very Protestant in its perspective, so please don't be offended if you're Catholic or an Easterner. I am also intentionally highlighting the negative aspects of our religion to make a point.

AD 0-33: A Palestinian Jew named Jesus of Nazareth lived, taught, and demonstrated the coming of what he called the kingdom of God. He confronted the establishments, loved the sinners, healed the sick people, and then died as a sacrifice for the sins of all generations. Then he disappeared into the clouds, much to the disappointment of his followers.

AD 33¼: The Holy Spirit came with great power, and the disciples finally realized what the whole enchilada was about.

AD 34-100: The original 11 disciples—plus Judas' replacement, along with about 500 or so others—had some pretty radical years of fruitful ministry. They continued to teach what Jesus taught, along with stories of what he'd done. Mostly they stuck close to Israel, but then a new convert named Paul got his fingers in the pie and they started going to some exotic places: Turkey, Africa, Greece, and even north into Europe. It was a good-news-and-bad-news time. Many accepted this teaching of salvation and a new way to live; yet many also faced persecution, torture, and execution.

AD 100-313: The message of Jesus' kingdom spread through the Middle East, North Africa, Turkey, and Greece—basically the whole Roman world. For every Christ-follower who was killed, 10 more seemingly popped out of the ground to take his or her place. A few emperors and religious leaders apparently embraced this new concept of living life in relationship with the Creator, but many were repulsed by this growing demographic and its potential threat to the systems they had worked so hard to build. During this period, people began to wander from the original teachings of Jesus. Rules and regulations began replacing the living daily relationship with the Spirit of God. A new religion called "Christianity" was born.

AD 313: The Roman emperor Constantine decided to make the religion of the Christians legal, and it later became the official religion of the expanding Western world. His decision was more political than personal, as Constantine continued to favor Mars and Apollo with his own offerings. That is, until one night in a dream he heard instructions to put the sign of the cross upon his soldiers' shields. After a victory, Constantine decided that the credit belonged to the God of the Christians and committed himself—at least in the public view—to the "Christian faith."

AD 313-1550: This new religion, Christianity, which was loosely based on the Bible and had very little to do with what Jesus said or did, expanded everywhere. Emperors and kings became religious dictators, killing any dissenters, forcing arbitrary conversion on people, clamping a title on them for the sake of political unity or military conscription. Somewhere within this time frame, people began to take the Greek word *ekklesia* and use it as a place-name noun: "the church."

During this time, every few years, one radical preacher or another would get a hold on a pulpit and use his 15 minutes of fame to call the people back to the teachings of Jesus. Usually these figures faced excommunication or death for their pains. Many who didn't die moved to the hinterlands to build places of retreat, typically called monasteries.

The Renaissance, which occurred near the end of this period, was similar in its inception to Christianity in that it got some things right. The thinking of this period arose from appreciating the dignity of humanity, the discoveries of science and nature, and the capacity of the mind and talents God gave humans. Good stuff.

But generally speaking, people were confused about who was worshipping what. Then, in 1517, a Catholic priest by the name of Martin Luther entered the scene. He realized that this thing called Christianity was a big mess and in need of an overhaul. So he wrote a list of 95 things that should be fixed. Guess what? Hardly anybody appreciated it. In the same way that Jesus didn't found the religion of Christianity, Luther didn't found the Protestant faith. He didn't want a new religion. He wanted to see some things changed within the Catholic system so he could conscientiously remain in it.

AD 1700: The period known as the Enlightenment arrived. In some ways it continued where the Renaissance left off. People placed humanity at the center of the universe and put renewed emphasis on the power of the mind. In fact, people liked themselves so much that they practically built whole nations out of ideologies. The "individual" was supreme—giving rise to the idea of "individual human rights," a concept never conceived before. The later developments of representative government, religious freedom, and civil rights resulted from the thinking of the Enlightenment philosophers during this period.

AD 1800: The West expanded farther west, deeply south, and even to the Far East, conquering with the assistance of technology produced by the so-called Enlightenment. God, gold, and glory dominated the period. From 1550 to 1850, the religion of Christianity divided and split into many different brand names. The original protesters had since dispersed into hundreds of types of Protestants. In fact, Protestantism seemed to thrive in the newly individualistic Western world. Protestants considered it an obligation to carry the gospel with them to the New World, zealously converting the natives to Christianity.

We can be sure, both through historical perspectives and firsthand accounts, that men of the cloth did honestly share the truth of Jesus in spite of the invasions they may have been part of but were never party to.

AD 1850-1900: This was the time of the thinkers Sigmund Freud, Karl Marx, Charles Darwin, and Friedrich Nietzsche. Four brilliant, edgy, ahead-of-their-time philosophers. Each one, in his own way, summarized "religion" as the easy way out for weaklings. Humanity was the answer. They asserted that we must be our own saviors, and that the answer is in economics, psychology, science, and philosophy.

AD 1920 to the present day: The religion of Christianity has experienced a significant awakening. Fundamentalism, Pentecostalism, evangelicalism, and the various renewal groups have all but redefined what it means to be a "Christian." These groups tend to be Bible-centered and worship oriented. Some are "Spirit filled." There's even been a gradual return to talking directly about Jesus again. But still, we have some scary questions to ponder...

What influence have all the different eras, philosophers, governments, and histories had on this thing we call "Christianity"?

Is the modern system really built on the life and teachings of Jesus of Nazareth, or is it a complicated conglomeration of ideas and flaws from different centuries and different perspectives?

Where did Jesus go in the bigger picture?

As I look over the history of Christendom, I notice our minds are where our hearts should be. The kingdom of Jesus has somehow become a religion of the mind rather than a spiritual response of the heart. We focus on psychological compliance rather than spiritual dependence upon the teachings of Jesus and the guidance of the Comforter, the Holy Spirit.

#sharejesus:

The kingdom of Jesus has somehow become a religion of the mind rather than a spiritual response of the heart.

41. It's All About Grace and Truth

Christianity has problems, in so many ways. While the ideals of Christianity have a basis in Jesus, in the history of the world—from the Crusades to Calvin's oppression of Geneva—we have often seen everything but Jesus' love. Culturally, Christianity has met with resistance because of this pained history, and also because, to most of the world, embracing Christianity means embracing Western civilization, Western policy, and even Western rule.

Even within the boundaries of our own "civilized" countries, we can see the systemic problems within Christianity. Picketers, political manipulators, and cultural warmongers all tend to have their own versions of Christianity. Many racists consider themselves Christians. The same goes for many corrupt politicians, gangsters, and abusive parents.

The coin has another side, too. Within the domain of Christianity, we all suffer beneath the weight of sin. Understanding the doctrine of forgiveness does not deliver us from sin. Jesus does. Our Western logic, our reason, our "right thinking" cannot deliver us from evil.

John, known as "the disciple whom Jesus loved," wrote, "For the law was given through Moses; grace and truth came through Jesus Christ" (John 1:17). Rather than maintaining his Jewish allegiance to the laws of Moses, John chose to live in the grace of Jesus, taking the truth of Jesus' love as his foremost identity.

Grace and truth must be our focus—and both of those huge words are rooted in what Jesus said and did. The way forward is to know what he said and did better than we know right now—then we'll have some grace and truth to share with others.

#sharejesus:

The way forward is to know what Jesus said and did better than we know right now.

42. Focus on What You Have to Give, Not How Others Respond

Sometimes we're "persecuted" for our faith not because of the message we're hoping people will receive, but because we're not very "human" in the way we talk about Jesus. He was *both* God and human, remember—that means he excelled at relating to other humans.

And sometimes others have trouble with our message simply because they misconstrue Christ's love and forgiveness for them— they assume judgment is his priority, and don't know that he said: "For God did not send his Son into the world to condemn the world, but to save the world through him" (John 3:17).

Looking at the life of Jesus, we can surely agree that his delivery was always suited for the time and the person. He was angry in the Temple. He was abundantly gracious with a woman caught in adultery. He was slightly less grace-filled with his disciples. Tougher on Peter than on Andrew. Downright mean to the Pharisees. He asked nothing of the healed lepers and the blind and the beggars. He delivered without question the demoniacs and hassled his disciples when they showed little or no faith.

The delivery of Jesus' good news—that the kingdom of God had arrived—changed nearly every time he presented it. But let's assume he always did it right. Were there times the recipients of his message couldn't hear? So many times. The disciples constantly confused his message with their version of politics. They believed Jesus would restore the physical kingdom of Israel.

The Pharisees, Sadducees, and Herodians heard Jesus attacking their power base. The Roman leaders heard Jesus wanting to overthrow their empire.

The ones who truly had ears to hear Jesus typically were the hurting, the broken, the desperate. What united the misunderstandings of the disciples, the religious leaders, and the political leaders was an inability to hear the message of the kingdom the way Jesus presented it. They all heard *power*. Either that Jesus was about to give them earthly power or that he wanted to take it away. He was speaking of a whole new way—but they couldn't hear because their ears were clogged with the ways of the world.

And in the end, Jesus died because of this message. Some of the people *did* understand what he was saying and realized that it was, in fact, a threat to their way of life. So they crucified him. And Jesus was kind enough to warn us that if the world's powerbrokers treated him this way, we should expect similar treatment at times.

It helps to know that our only responsibility is to give our "good treasure"—the incredible invitation of Jesus to know him and love him—to those we meet. We can't do much of anything about how people choose to interpret the "good news" we're bringing, unless we're offering it in a formulaic, non-human sort of way. Be yourself, and give what you have to give. That's all you can hope to do.

#sharejesus:

Looking at the life of Jesus, we can surely agree that his delivery was always suited for the time and the person.

43. Make It About Jesus, Not About Doctrine

Doctrine is a set of beliefs taught by the church about God and the Bible. Doctrine is a good thing. We all have doctrines—things we believe. They may not be well-thought-through, but we have them. We believe something about almost everything. However, where we go terribly off course is *when we make a conversation about doctrine rather than Jesus himself.*

Several years ago I met with a group of Lebanese doctors. All Muslims. We were in one of their houses and reading through the book of Luke. A new doctor, a friend of the one whose house we were in, showed up in the middle of one such evening. He was surprised to find a group of his friends sitting around reading the Bible with an American guy. Before he really knew what was going on, he blurted out, pointing at me, "This man is a Christian and believes Jesus was crucified; how can you be reading the Bible with him?"

After he said this, everyone looked straight at me, waiting for an answer. Partly because I was dumbfounded, and partly because I have learned to wait in such situations, I didn't say anything. After what seemed like an eternity—probably 5 seconds—the host said to his friend: "How about you just come on in and sit down. We were having a good discussion before you came in and interrupted."

His friend, embarrassed, sat down. We went on. Luke chapter 3. I never said a word. Didn't answer. Didn't defend. And the man ended up joining our group. Did I agree with him? No. We did have different doctrines. We did not agree. But fighting over doctrine at that time would have been a huge error. The quicker we can get past the necessity of talking about our beliefs and, instead, talk about Jesus, the better off we'll be. Maybe doctrine will matter later on—probably it will—but that's way down the road.

#sharejesus:

Where we go terribly off course is when we make a conversation about doctrine rather than Jesus himself.

44. Avoid Christianese, Please!

Here's a truth about basic communication: "It's not what I say that matters, but what you hear." Over the course of 2,000 years, Christianity has developed its very own language, including different dialects. We call it Christianese. Every time a branch group or new denomination develops, it creates its own unique personality, including its own diction: specific terms and keywords and catch phrases, all with varying levels of importance.

Some of this terminology is helpful; some of it is not. Some of it is correct; some of it is downright unbiblical. Somewhere, in the combination of these terms, words become packed with meanings and implications—useful and otherwise. As the joke goes, when the old-time preacher asked the sinner on the side of the road, "Are you washed in the blood?" the confused man looked at himself to check and replied, "I sure hope not."

Clearly, an example of correct terminology that is not helpful.

I hate to be the one to say it, but maybe we need a "word police." We can mount lights and sirens on hats and pull people over when they use one of the unhelpful or incorrect words. We could even write tickets, impose fines, put people in the pillory, and throw tomatoes and cabbage and pomegranates at them. In love, of course.

We could have a verbal inquisition of sorts, and we could have a secret handshake and decoder rings. "Halt!" we could shout at people when they're busted. "On your knees, hands behind your back. Now repeat after me, 'I will not speak Christianese around other human beings, and if I do so, I will be infested with the fleas of a thousand llamas.' " So, because we're all likely unaware of how often we use words and phrases that sound weird to those who don't speak Christianese, let's be hyper-aware of how we refer to things. Let's slow down and consider how we can use regular, everyday words to describe the truths of Jesus.

#sharejesus:

Repeat after me: "I will not speak Christianese around other human beings."

45. Describe Rather Than Label

I invited a young Muslim guy by the name of Ahmed to come to the community center I'd started in Beirut, and he was instantly curious. "What is it called?" he asked. "The Olive Grove," I said. "It's a community of faith where people from all kinds of religious backgrounds can come together to find meaning in loving each other and following God." Suspicious, he asked, "So it's a church?" I answered, "Not at all, and what do you mean by *church*?" He said: "You know, like the Catholics. Are you a priest?" I said: "No, but, we have some Catholics who come to the Olive Grove. And many Muslims, too. You'll just have to come check it out sometime. We meet on Friday nights, and basically we are trying to learn how to get along with each other and how to get along with God. We've been studying the life of Jesus, and trying to learn from him."

"Aha!" he said. "So you are a Christian. You believe in Jesus!" I answered, "No, not really." I paused for a second. "Do the Christians you know live and act like Jesus?"

He looked around, then said: "Well, no. Not really." I asked, "Do you think Jesus was a Christian?" He answered, "Of course." Then he scratched his head. "Or maybe he was a Muslim."

I don't have a great replacement word for *church*. So I propose an experiment. The next time you want to invite someone to participate with you in your spiritual journey, instead of *calling* it a small group or a church group, *describe* what you do. Say that you and your friends are meeting to learn and you're discussing Jesus and his teachings. Leave it at that, unless your friend wants to know what else you do. If so, describe the fun stuff and the great people who are part of your group. "Church" carries with it so much baggage that it's hard to get past all that when you're wanting to invite someone into your community.

#sharejesus:

We are trying to learn how to get along with each other and how to get along with God.

46. Living the Jesus Way

What makes Jesus so attractive? Jesus' way was not religious. Jesus knew how to work within the religious boundaries of the time, without becoming religious himself. His teaching centered on bringing the prophecies of the Old Testament to bear upon himself. His parables and stories were illustrations of the kingdom of heaven. Jesus' ease within the religious system came from his confidence. He knew who he was. This gave him great power and freedom, an ability to be comfortable in any part of the world, and yet not be of it. Jesus didn't start a new religion called Christianity. He lived in relationship, and he extended relationship. This was Jesus' way.

Jesus' way was patient and kind. A quick glance at the New Testament tells us it took his closest disciples three years with Jesus and then the events of Pentecost before they understood, before they really knew what was going on. And yet, during his three years of ministry, we see Jesus' impatience with the disciples only once or twice, and not because of a lack of progress—because of a lack of faith. Jesus lived as an example of extraordinary patience. Throughout the Gospels, we see the disciples repeatedly asking dumb questions, making mistakes, and endlessly jockeying for positions in a kingdom they couldn't dream of. Yet Jesus was kind to them, despite their immaturity. In fact, regardless of their hitches and glitches, Jesus encouraged his followers to take part in the discipleship of others.

When we attempt to live in the way of Jesus, we'll feel like the mission is too big for us, the same way that even his closest disciples felt before us. But that's actually a good thing—living in the way of Jesus will force us to depend on him when we do. And when we're depending on Jesus, talking to others about him is not such a big deal. They'll likely be attracted by, or at least intrigued by, the way you're living. That will create lots of opportunities to tell them why.

#sharejesus:

Jesus knew that giving his friends an unimaginably huge task would require their reliance on him and inspire their passions.

47. Friending the Untouchables

I recently read the book *Jesus Before Christianity,* by a priest named Albert Nolan. He points out how Jesus differed from other figures of his time by mixing socially with all kinds of people. "John the Baptist preached to sinners," he writes, "Hanina ben Dosa exorcised evil spirits from them. But Jesus identified with them. He went out of his way to mix socially with beggars, tax collectors and prostitutes."[6]

Nolan goes on to describe how dining with company was the ultimate in social intimacy. It was impolite in the society of the time, and perhaps even to this day, to dine with lower classes, or to entertain someone whose lifestyle was disapproved of. Jesus constantly violated this obvious social taboo. Nolan writes: "The scandal Jesus caused in that society by mixing socially with sinners can hardly be imagined by most people in the modern world today. It meant that he accepted them and approved of them and that he actually wanted to be 'a friend of tax collectors and sinners.' "[7]

Can you imagine what that would look like today? Instead of promoting our doctrines and beliefs, what if we started inviting our culture's versions of "tax collectors and sinners" into our community activities and our friend groups and our houses? When we reach out to the untouchables in our culture—even in tiny, safe ways—we are living in the Spirit of Jesus. And when we do, we are speaking of Jesus through our actions, rather than just our words.

#sharejesus:

Jesus went out of his way to mix socially with beggars, tax collectors, and prostitutes.

48. Always Default to Jesus

One of the first challenges you'll encounter as you begin to share your wonderful friendship with Jesus is someone saying something like: "Are you trying to tell me that Jesus is the only way? That the pygmies in Africa are going to hell because they don't know Jesus? And what about my Buddhist friend who is, well, a lot nicer than you—and who never tells me that I'm going to hell or that I have it wrong? Huh?"

First of all, you would say: "I don't think I told you that you were going anywhere, let alone hell. And I also don't think I mentioned anything about Jesus being the only way, or anything about pygmies or Buddhists. But other than that...." But you will definitely have people get all uncomfortable with you, simply because you're speaking of Jesus—even if you're doing it in the nicest, friendliest way. They will hear the name "Jesus" come out of your mouth. And they will assume a bunch of things based on stuff they've heard in the past.

As always, you have choices. You can simply say, "Yep, sorry, He's the only way." Fair enough. That's still the truth. But there are two problems with the "Yep, he's the only way" approach: One is that Jesus himself typically didn't use that tactic. The other is that it's a door-closer, which is possibly why Jesus used it so seldom. Remember that just because something is true doesn't mean you need to say it right away in a conversation. It might be true that I have a paunch—a little overweight, let's say. But if you introduce yourself to me and then say, "By the way, Carl, you're a bit chubby," that just wouldn't be helpful—although maybe true.

Or you can go to the other extreme and say something like: "Yeah, you're right, and who really knows anyway? Maybe all roads do lead to God." Now if that's what you believe, I'd challenge you to read the Book again to see if you're on the right track with that argument. Or some might think like I do—that Jesus is the only way—but you just don't want to say it. I'd call that being a chicken. You can strategically delay the answer, which I have often done, but you can't ultimately ignore it or pretend this issue doesn't exist. For many people, how we answer this question determines whether they'll keep listening to what we have to say.

The best way to answer in a non-chickeny way, I think, is to simply bring it back to Jesus. He's the one who said this: "I am the way and the truth and the life. No one comes to the Father except through me" (John 14:6). You love and follow Jesus, and that's what he said. It's a hard thing to swallow in a diverse culture, but Jesus said lots of other hard things, too. Move the conversation from what you *believe* to what Jesus *said*—that's a neutral place to launch into it.

#sharejesus:

You will definitely have people get all uncomfortable with you, simply because you're speaking of Jesus.

49. Admit That Jesus Confuses You Sometimes, Too

If Jesus dropped by to talk, he would completely outwit me. He proved himself to the most capable minds in Jerusalem—why do I assume that I'm more qualified because I know a few things about the Bible? If I experienced Jesus the way the disciples did, I would be every bit as silly and moronic and confused and unreasonable as Peter and the others. Jesus would baffle me completely. Come to think of it, he often does.

One minute we're not supposed to be angry, not supposed to even think about lusting; we're supposed to love our enemies, pray for terrible people, and yet we're not supposed to practice righteousness in front of people—so they won't notice? I'm a bit confused. If you loved your enemies, didn't lust, and didn't get angry with people, you would stick out like a sore thumb.

He even said that our prayer lives should be a secret between God and us. The truest prayer is the one said earnestly when we are alone with God. When we pray overtly in front of others, it is easy to derail the genuine communion of our hearts before God and replace it with something that sounds nice, something that others want to hear or think impressive. And Jesus commands forgiveness toward others as a key component of being forgiven ourselves. In fact, he said, "If you do not forgive men their sins, your Father will not forgive your sins" (Matthew 6:15).

It's okay that we don't know the answers to every question—neither did any of his disciples. When you're asked questions you can't answer, simply acknowledge that truth, then offer to explore the answer together.

#sharejesus:

It's okay that we don't know the answers to every question—neither did any of his disciples.

50. Jesus Himself

On a visit to my friend Ted's house not long ago, he was pacing, deep in thought. Finally, he looked up at me and said: "I really don't think modern Christianity needs anything...except Jesus."

"Yeah," I said, "and boy do we need a lot of him."

I'm not one of those people who have a lot of light-bulb moments. I don't sit underneath trees on the mountaintops and contemplate the meaning of life. I don't burn incense in my office or meditate three hours a day. But I have spent most of the last two decades talking about Jesus, and you can't do something like that for such a long time without some of it actually hitting home.

When I first started my career as a missionary, I was full of ideas. I had a message so big it took a moving company to transport it. During 20 years of sharing my faith, I learned that there's really only one thing that's important, and that is Jesus himself. Whatever you do, and whatever you think you're supposed to do, it all comes back to Jesus himself. Pay more attention to him than you have before, and talk about him just a little more than you have in the past. You'll leave something like a trail of breadcrumbs behind you in your life—little tastes of Jesus that others will find, eat, and then crave some more.

Your friends, and your enemies, are hungry for that bread—and they might not even know it. Scatter what you have for them. Some of them will be so grateful you did.

#sharejesus:

After years of sharing my faith, I learned that there's really only one thing that's important, and that is Jesus himself.

ENDNOTES

[1] Todd M. Johnson, David B. Barrett, and Peter F. Crossing. "Christianity 2011: Martyrs and the Resurgence of Religion," International Bulletin of Missionary Research 35, No. 1 (January 2011), 29.

[2] Ibid.

[3] E. Stanley Jones, *The Christ of the Indian Road* (Nashville: Abingdon, 1925), 12.

[4] Ibid.

[5] Ibid.

[6] Albert Nolan, *Jesus Before Christianity* (Maryknoll, NY: Orbis, 2001), 45.

[7] Ibid.